prayers&promises
for
mothers

Rachel Quillin
and
Nancy J. Farrier

BARBOUR
PUBLISHING

*Our mission is to publish and distribute inspirational products offer-
ing exceptional value and biblical encouragement to the masses.*

Member of the
Evangelical Christian
Publishers Association

Contents

PREFACE

Motherhood is one of God's most precious blessings. It brings much joy and fills the heart with a new and special kind of love.

Even though the life of a mother is filled with joy, love, and all manner of happiness, it often contains fears, doubts, and questions. At times, the demands can be overwhelming, but God does not expect mothers to accomplish their tasks alone. His Word is filled with many promises. Some of them are specific to parenting, and others can certainly be applied.

The pages of this book are filled with many of these wonderful promises, accompanied by prayers for any mother to pray. It is our hope that you will draw comfort from these words and will begin to claim God's promises for your own life. It is our prayer that your personal time of fellowship with the heavenly Father will be a source of strength and encouragement to you.

A Quiet Response

*A soft answer turneth away wrath:
but grievous words stir up anger.*

PROVERBS 15:1

Sometimes, Father, when I'm cleaning up one mess, my kids are in the next room making an even bigger mess. I want to scream—and sometimes I do. But, Lord, I know that only makes the situation worse. The kids get worked up, and I just get more upset. Help me to be calm as I deal with these frustrations and to keep in mind that a quiet response will get greater results.

I should know from experience. When I've made a mess of things, You've spoken gently through Your Word and through the Holy Spirit. I know I like that better than a screaming, belittling voice. Remind me that my children would prefer that as well.

DON'T BE A FOOL

Be not hasty in thy spirit to be angry:
for anger resteth in the bosom of fools.

ECCLESIASTES 7:9

Lord, probably the last thing I want to be is a fool. But I'm afraid that in my anger I've made my foolishness clear on more than one occasion.

I don't like to be angry with my children, Father. Certainly some of what they do needs to be corrected, but there's a right way and a wrong way to handle this. I guess the old adage "Two wrongs don't make a right" could be applied here. My lashing out doesn't counteract their mistakes; it only confirms my own foolishness. My behavior says that hasty anger is an appropriate response when something upsets them; it doesn't demonstrate how to properly handle frustration. Guide me, Father, to correct them without becoming angry.

CEASE FROM ANGER

Cease from anger, and forsake wrath:
fret not thyself in any wise to do evil.

PSALM 37:8

Dear God, I have to admit that on the surface this often seems like an impossible command to obey. I have ideals in my head about how my children should act, how much time I should spend with my husband, and so forth. When things don't go the way I plan, I snap. I take my anger out on anything and everything. Lord, my plans might actually be reasonable, but I know that doesn't give me an excuse to be angry when interruptions occur.

I know that You wouldn't have told me to "cease from anger" if You didn't expect me to do it. And just as with other seemingly impossible tasks, I know that You will give me the strength I need when I need it. Thank You, Father.

RESOLVING ANGER TODAY

Be ye angry, and sin not:
let not the sun go down upon your wrath.

EPHESIANS 4:26

God, I'm sure that in my foolishness I've caused You plenty of reason to be angry. But You know how to handle anger, and too many times I don't. If one of my children disobeys, I have a hard time controlling my temper. Too often I harbor anger throughout the day. All I want is for us to go to bed so we can start fresh the next day.

But, Lord, instead of waiting until tomorrow, You want me to start fresh today—before the sun goes down. You know that will help our whole family. Please help me keep that in mind. Lend me a hand so I can handle anger the way You do. Help me not to lose my temper with my children or my husband, and give me the grace to forgive—today.

A REWARD FROM GOD

Children are an heritage of the LORD:
and the fruit of the womb is his reward.

PSALM 127:3

You've given me a lovely reward, dear Father. I know that my children actually belong to You, and I need to treat them in that way. Along with the privilege of being a mother, I've been given the great responsibility of teaching my children, using the guidelines You've established in Your Word.

Please help me not to squander this great opportunity. I want to please You by taking utmost care of this wonderful reward that You've bestowed on me. I want to nurture these children both physically and spiritually. My desire is that others would realize I truly understand my children came from You and that I've given them back to You. Please continue to bless this family. Thank You, Jesus.

Blessings for My Children

I will pour water upon him that is thirsty,
and floods upon the dry ground:
I will pour my spirit upon thy seed,
and my blessing upon thine offspring.

Isaiah 44:3

You have certainly packed Your Word with promises, Father. Right now I'd like to claim the ones in Isaiah 44:3. Oh, how I desire to see my children filled with Your Holy Spirit! I want them to serve You and to experience the blessings that You want to shower upon them.

Lord Jesus, draw my family close to You. Fill our home with Your presence and our lives with Your love. In turn, help each one of us to realize the importance of blessing others. You have given us so much, but still, each day we need to be drawn closer to You. Instill that desire within our hearts. And thank You for Your many blessings!

A MAN FROM THE LORD

Adam knew Eve his wife;
and she conceived, and bare Cain, and said,
I have gotten a man from the LORD.

GENESIS 4:1

Lord, from the moment I was aware of each child growing in my womb, I knew that each was from You. How could I ever doubt that such miracles could come from any source other than You?

As each child entered this world, I couldn't help but praise You for this wonderful gift You granted to me. Through the joys and struggles of motherhood, I've been able to rest in the truth that these children are indeed from You, and because of Your goodness I've received them. Thank You, Lord, that in Your perfect plan You've seen fit to give me beautiful children whom I probably don't deserve. Thank You for allowing me to be a mother. That is truly a gift from You.

WISE CHILDREN

*Better is a poor and a wise child
than an old and foolish king,
who will no more be admonished.*

ECCLESIASTES 4:13

My children aren't wealthy, Father—at least not by the world's standards. It's not too likely that they ever will be as long as they're relying on their parents for their income. I wouldn't say they're poor either; but, of course, these aren't the things that matter. Listening to and heeding wise counsel will make them far better people than either wealth or poverty.

Please give me the wisdom I need to properly advise my children. Help me teach them to seek guidance from Your Word and in communion with the Holy Spirit. I might not be able to offer earthly riches, but I can teach them Your truths, and that's what really counts. As my children grow, Lord, help them to use wisdom.

REACHING OUT TO OTHERS

Finally, be ye all of one mind,
having compassion one of another,
love as brethren,
be pitiful, be courteous.

1 PETER 3:8

You know, Father, sometimes I'm guilty of feeling sorry for myself, but when I stop and really think about why I'm complaining, I realize that I have much to be thankful for. There are so many people who really do need a listening ear or a heartfelt hug.

Often, Lord, it's my own children who need a mother's compassionate arms. It's sometimes hard to reach out to others, including my kids, because I feel so vulnerable. I'm afraid I'll say or do the wrong thing. But You want me to extend myself to the hurting individuals in this world, and I know You'll show me what to do.

Please, Father, help me to never turn down an opportunity to offer compassion.

MAKING A DIFFERENCE

And of some have compassion,
making a difference.

JUDE 22

What a long way a little compassion goes, dear Jesus. Sometimes I think that all I need is a hug to make me feel better. I'm sure that others out there feel the same way. It's obvious that my kids often do.

Just the other day my little one hurt himself. I was busy and could have easily told him to sit and rest a few minutes and he'd be okay. Physically that might have been true, but he would only have become frustrated. What a joy it was for me to sit with him and to see the healing powers of a mother's compassion. How quickly he recovered!

Lord, sometimes compassion is all a person needs to gain strength. I pray I will always offer it freely.

COMPASSION
IN PLACE OF ANGER

He, being full of compassion,
forgave their iniquity, and destroyed them not:
yea, many a time turned he his anger away,
and did not stir up all his wrath.

PSALM 78:38

Dear God, if You can set Your wrath aside and, instead, offer forgiving compassion for my abundant sins, how can I do less when it concerns the errors of my children and even other people? You've been so gracious when I didn't deserve it! I need Your strength to be compassionate when someone wrongs me. It's easier for me to strike back, but I want to be like You.

I know it's important that I do this, not only for the feelings of everyone involved but also so that I might be an example of Your love. I wouldn't want to be responsible for anyone, especially my children, rejecting You because I chose to react inappropriately to a wrong done. Please direct my actions, Lord.

Unfailing Compassion

*It is of the LORD's mercies
that we are not consumed,
because his compassions fail not.
They are new every morning:
great is thy faithfulness.*

Thank You, Lord, for being so faithful. Thank You that each day Your compassion for me is just the right amount to get me through the day. Some mornings I don't even want to open my eyes; I close them tight, hoping to squeeze out the fact that there is an unending number of tasks that await me.

I don't want to face the inevitable sibling fights that are just around the corner. For that matter, I don't want to think of the early ordeal of trying to come up with a breakfast that my kids will actually eat.

When I face it from my perspective, I'm overwhelmed, but when I remember that You are offering me Your compassion, I am renewed. I rejoice in Your faithfulness.

GREAT GAIN

Godliness with contentment is great gain.

1 TIMOTHY 6:6

Lord, sometimes I see great gain as something to be obtained from worldly achievement. I even teach my children this when I praise them more for scholastic, artistic, or sport success than I do for their faith in You. Sometimes I long to hear the praise of people for the job I do when I should be concerned with doing what pleases You.

Show me how to be a godly woman, how to have true contentment that comes from service to You, Jesus. I don't want to gratify selfish desires. Help me to reinforce in my home the need to be satisfied with doing Your will. That contentment will bring great gain to my family and will be a lasting blessing for generations to come.

NEVER FORSAKEN

Let your conversation be without covetousness;
and be content with such things as ye have:
for he hath said, I will never leave thee,
nor forsake thee.

HEBREWS 13:5

What an amazing promise, Lord! I want to always be there for my children, but I know there may be a time when I won't be around. It's such a comfort to me to know that You will never leave them, just as You've never left me. You will never turn Your back on any of us, no matter what we do.

Help me to rejoice in the time I have with my family today. I don't want to dwell on what might happen in the future; I want to relish this chance to nurture and cherish the blessings You've given me. Thank You that I can be content—not longing for what I don't have or looking for something more. I can rest in the assurance that You are here now and will be in the future.

WANTING NOTHING

Not that I speak in respect of want:
for I have learned, in whatsoever state I am,
therewith to be content.

PHILIPPIANS 4:11

Father, some days I want so many things—I feel like a little child, stomping my foot and demanding my way. At the time, all those desires seem so necessary; yet when I stop to think, I know they don't truly matter. They are material and temporal and of no value in heaven.

How can I tell my children to be happy with what they have when I always want more from You? Fill me with so much contentment that my family will be blessed with understanding this principle. Teach us to be satisfied with Your provision for our needs. Help me realize that my wants are temporary and of little importance. Let me lean against You, Lord, relaxed in the knowledge that You will care for me.

SATISFIED WITH GOODNESS

Blessed is the man whom thou choosest,
and causest to approach unto thee,
that he may dwell in thy courts:
we shall be satisfied with the goodness of
thy house, even of thy holy temple.

PSALM 65:4

I did it again, Lord. Someone at church said something to hurt my feelings. I was polite until I got home, but then my hurt and anger boiled over. I can still see the wide eyes of my children as they listened to my unkind words. How could I have listed my complaints in front of them? I should have talked to You in private. Forgive me, Father.

Give me the wisdom to talk with my family about what I said. Maybe that person at church wasn't feeling well. Maybe I misunderstood the intended meaning. After all, how many times have I allowed something to slip off my tongue without thinking?

I want to show my children the value of self-control and forgiveness within the church family. Help us to see others the way You see them.

GOING THE RIGHT WAY

Train up a child in the way he should go:
and when he is old, he will not depart from it.

PROVERBS 22:6

Lord, I know Your Word says not to worry, but I can't seem to help it. I tried to train my children right, but I have one who is making some bad choices. I'm afraid this child is getting away from You, Lord.

Isaiah 55:11 says that Your Word won't return to You void but will accomplish its purpose. Help me to trust that the Scriptures we memorized together and the discipline and training I gave my child will keep him going the right way. Bring to his remembrance those verses and memories of discipline when I can't be there. Don't let him escape the truth.

I know you desire that none will perish—even wayward children. Thank You, Lord, that You care even more than I do.

DOING AS GOD DOES

Thou shalt also consider in thine heart, that,
as a man chasteneth his son,
so the LORD thy God chasteneth thee.

DEUTERONOMY 8:5

Thank You, Lord, for setting the example for me
as a parent. There are times when I haven't listened,
when I've done what I wanted to do, and You have
chastened me. It hurt, Lord, but I learned a valuable lesson.

Disciplining my children isn't fun. Sometimes
I want to be lenient when I shouldn't be. Then
there are times when I want to be firmer than I
should be. Help me to keep the seriousness of the
sin in mind. I need to remember that I also have
needed reproof. Give me compassion along with
the strong stand I need to take.

After the chastening is over, remind me to
give them a hug and tell them how much I love
them, just as You demonstrate Your love for me.

LOVING CHASTISEMENT

*As many as I love,
I rebuke and chasten:
be zealous therefore, and repent.*

REVELATION 3:19

Lord, this doesn't feel like love. When I look in those big eyes filled with tears, I don't want to follow through with any discipline. I want to smile, hug them, and tell them that all is forgiven. But, there are consequences for sin, and my children need to learn that now while they're young.

The world has a perverted view of love. Some say that you are showing your love if you give material possessions to your children and allow them to do as they please. Your Word says something different, Lord.

I want to love the way You do. I want to be strong, to lovingly discipline my children so they will grow to be pleasing to You. No matter how difficult it is, I will chastise with love.

Peaceable Fruit

Now no chastening for the present seemeth to be joyous, but grievous: nevertheless afterward it yieldeth the peaceable fruit of righteousness unto them which are exercised thereby.

Hebrews 12:11

Lord, I can't thank You enough for the promise and truth found in Your Word. I would not have believed it possible for my child to have such a change of heart. Yesterday she was a terror. Nothing would please her. Today she's the sweetest, most loving child a parent could want.

I know that once again the sinful nature will rear its ugly head. My beautiful child will become willful and demanding. She'll want her way, not mine or Yours. I also know that the discipline won't be joyous. It will hurt; however, Your promise will hold true once more. Thank You that Your Word is right every time, Lord. Each time my child tests the boundaries, I can throw up the fence You provide.

HOLDING HANDS

*I the LORD thy God will hold thy right hand,
saying unto thee,
Fear not; I will help thee.*

ISAIAH 41:13

I watched my children today, Lord—one afraid, the other reaching out a hand to help the fearful one. Tears came to my eyes as I thought of all the times that You've been there for me when I was afraid. You've held my hand and helped me in some difficult situations. With Your help I've walked when I might have fallen.

Not once have You ever laughed at me or told me how silly I was to be fearful. Lord, sometimes the things my children are uncertain about seem so unimportant to me. I struggle not to laugh. Help me to be understanding, to encourage rather than discourage. I want to take their hands and walk with them, as You've taken mine to walk with me.

Promise of Forever

When I saw him, I fell at his feet as dead.
And he laid his right hand upon me,
saying unto me, Fear not;
I am the first and the last:
I am he that liveth, and was dead;
and, behold, I am alive for evermore, Amen;
and have the keys of hell and of death.

Revelation 1:17–18

Lord, my children are bombarded with false religions: Islam, Buddhism, Hinduism. Every day we hear about tolerance and the need to accept others' beliefs. With all these differences being touted, it's hard to separate the truth. I want there to be no doubt about the truth.

Thank You for these verses. I can show my children that we serve a living God—not one who was here for a short time and then died. You conquered death. You hold the keys to hell and death. We have no need to fear either one.

Forever. Lord, what encouragement is in that word. We have all eternity to spend with You in heaven. Thank You for this indescribable gift. Thank You for being the Alpha and the Omega, the first and the last.

Held in God's Hand

Fear thou not; for I am with thee:
be not dismayed; for I am thy God:
I will strengthen thee; yea, I will help thee;
yea, I will uphold thee with the
right hand of my righteousness.

Isaiah 41:10

Today I don't want to go on, Lord. My friend is dying. Troubles are all around. My children look to me as an example, and I don't feel like I can carry on anymore.

Yet, I don't have to depend on my strength, because You give me Yours, Lord, and You never run out. I can picture You holding me up as the difficulties press close. You help me when there is no one else to do so.

Thank You, Lord. I'm grateful that I can show my children where to turn in times of trouble. They don't have to try to do it all themselves, because we are all Your children. You care for us all and will carry us when times are tough. I praise You, Lord.

Being an Encourager

Now we exhort you, brethren,
warn them that are unruly,
comfort the feebleminded, support the weak,
be patient toward all men.

1 Thessalonians 5:14

Whether I like it or not, I am an example to my children, Lord. How many times have I failed to do what this verse commands? I'm not always patient. I don't take time to comfort or support those who need it most, and all the time my children are watching.

Day by day, moment by moment, I want to improve. I want to instruct my family on the need to be there for others, to encourage in whatever way is needed. Your Word says I have to do this by example.

The little ways count, Lord. Help me teach my children that to grow as encouragers they can start with small things as they comfort others and build from there.

BEING A ROLE MODEL

I will behave myself wisely in a perfect way.
O when wilt thou come unto me?
I will walk within my house with a perfect heart.

PSALM 101:2

Father, whether I like it or not, there are a lot of people out there vying for my kids' attention. They are exposed to many negative role models. First, Lord, I ask You to protect them. I want to limit the contact my children have with these sources of bad influence.

Even more importantly, guide me to be a good influence before my little ones and show them, even while they're very young, how important it is to walk in Your ways and to obey Your commands. Help me to live according to Your guidelines and thus show my kids that Your plan is best as they strive to live for You. Thank You, Lord.

A PATTERN TO FOLLOW

In all things shewing thyself
a pattern of good works:
in doctrine shewing uncorruptness,
gravity, sincerity, sound speech,
that cannot be condemned;
that he that is of the contrary part
may be ashamed,
having no evil thing to say of you.

TITUS 2:7–8

Lord Jesus, I belong to You. In my heart I know it, and to others I've proclaimed it. I want each area of my life to be an indication of that truth. With Your assistance my life can be a pattern for my children to follow. Through You, I can live a life that will give others no right to accuse me of any wrongdoing. I pray that You'll allow my life to be an example that will encourage my family, friends, and others to come to You.

Father, what a joy it would be for me to stand in Your presence and to hear You say that my life had been a pattern of Christlikeness that You were glad to have others see and follow.

PERFECTION

*Be ye therefore perfect,
even as your Father
which is in heaven is perfect.*

MATTHEW 5:48

Perfection. It's something I often doubt I can attain. It's true that I'd like for my kids to be perfect; I mean, who wouldn't? No one likes to think his or her child is so imperfect that the child might actually do something embarrassing.

I guess that must be how You feel, too, Lord. I'm sure my behavior has caused You embarrassment—even after You've told me in Your Word to be perfect. You gave Yourself as the example of whom I should follow. Guide me daily to commit to being perfect, as You are perfect. I know I can't expect my children to be perfect if I'm not willing to set the example. Help me as I strive to be like You.

LET THEM SEE JESUS IN ME

Hereunto were ye called:
because Christ also suffered for us,
leaving us an example,
that ye should follow his steps.

1 PETER 2:21

Dear Jesus, You are the best example of what a loving parent should be. I know I am called to be Christlike in all I do, and that includes my parenting methods.

Please give me the strength and the wisdom to be the godly example that my children need to see. I know that the life I live will have a profound influence on the attitudes my children develop concerning You.

I want to be instrumental in helping my kids establish a close walk with You. I realize that in order for this to happen I must be like You. Direct me daily to renew my commitment to follow in Your steps. Thank You for being the example I need.

GOD WILL PROVIDE

We walk by faith, not by sight.

2 CORINTHIANS 5:7

Dear Jesus, there are several mouths to feed, as well as bodies to clothe, in our family; and we are certainly not wealthy. Of course I am thankful for each member of my family, and I cannot complain about the cost of their food and clothing. I've no need to be concerned, because You have always met all our needs. Remind me that You will always provide when the supplies run low—right along with the cash.

Faith isn't easy when our minds are taught to believe only what we see; but faith *is* rewarding. It is better to walk by faith, because You will never fail us. What we see in this world does have the potential to fail us. So help me live by faith.

FAITH TO PROTECT
MY CHILDREN

By faith Moses, when he was born,
was hid three months of his parents,
because they saw he was a proper child;
and they were not afraid of
the king's commandment.

HEBREWS 11:23

What a wonderful example You have given me in Moses' parents. They faced the unbelievable command to kill their newborn son, but, Father, they knew You had a special plan for their child and that You would help them go against the king in this wicked situation.

Lord, I know You also have a special plan for my children. Help me to have the kind of faith Moses' parents had. I don't face the command to kill my children, but there are "experts" in powerful places who would have me go against Your Word in the way I raise my family. Give me the strength to stand strong and to abide in Your Word. Assist me in providing an environment that will allow my children to realize the plan You have for them.

WAITING FOR GOD

I will look unto the LORD;
I will wait for the God of my salvation:
my God will hear me.

MICAH 7:7

Waiting is not an easy thing, Father. I guess that seems especially true when I'm waiting for You to answer my prayers. Sometimes I find myself wondering if You've even heard my prayers.

When the baby swallowed something and we didn't know what it was, we were so afraid it would be harmful to her. We waited for the doctor to give us an answer, and we prayed that we would quickly know her condition. Hour after hour we waited without even seeing a doctor, much less hearing any news. It was hard, Lord. You knew our little girl was fine, but You wanted to remind us that our faith must be in You and that You will hear and answer our prayers in Your timing. Thank You for the reminder.

GREAT IS THY FAITH

*Then Jesus answered and said unto her,
O woman, great is thy faith:
be it unto thee even as thou wilt.*

MATTHEW 15:28

O Father, how I wish it could be said of me, "Great is thy faith," but I'm afraid I often fall short. The Canaanite mother had enough faith to realize that it would take just a small amount of Your power to heal her demon-possessed daughter.

I'm afraid that too many times my faith is so shallow that I believe what I need done is going to require an enormous amount of power. I may even convince myself that my need is not important enough to bother You with. In doing so, I miss receiving Your blessings. I know You promised in Matthew 17:20 that if I'd have faith the size of a mustard seed I'd be able to move a mountain with just a word. That's the kind of faith I want in my daily life.

THE COMFORT OF GOD

I, even I, am he that comforteth you:
who art thou, that thou shouldest be
afraid of a man that shall die,
and of the son of man which
shall be made as grass.

ISAIAH 51:12

Have You seen the news, Lord? Of course, You know everything that happens. I get so afraid. There are children killing children. I don't want to let mine out of my sight anymore; yet I know I can't protect them from the evils in the world.

As Abraham placed Isaac completely in Your care, help me to give You my children. I know that when I worry I keep taking them back. Take away my fear. Help me trust You with them every day.

Sometimes I can see my children watching me. They take their cue from how I react to negative news. Lord, remove the fears that bind me so that I can be happy in the knowledge that You are there to comfort me—no matter what is happening.

SHIELDED FROM FEAR

*After these things the word of the LORD
came unto Abram in a vision, saying,
Fear not, Abram:
I am thy shield,
and thy exceeding great reward.*

GENESIS 15:1

You are my shield, Lord. You both precede me
and follow me (see Psalm 139:5). You surround
me. I have nothing to fear. Who am I to deserve
such blessing from You? Sometimes I feel like
such a whiner, yet You respond by taking good
care of my family and me.

Let me understand the good kind of fear,
Father. I am in awe of You, but teach me how to
reverence You as You deserve. That way I can pass
this on to my children. Your Word says that perfect love casts out fear. Only by abiding in You all
the time do I find perfect love.

Thank You, Jesus. As we prayed together, I
could see the apprehension fading away. Peace once
more covers this house. Despite the outer turmoil,
my family and I will fear You and be delivered.

CONQUERING LOVE

*God hath not given us the spirit of fear;
but of power, and of love,
and of a sound mind.*

2 TIMOTHY 1:7

I hear a noise at night, and my heart pounds. The children cry when the lights are out. Someone makes a threat. There are gunshots. We hear horrible things on the news. I tremble inside when I think of what could happen. My little ones reflect my fear.

This isn't from You, Lord. This verse talks about power, love, and a sound mind. I know that those *are* from You. Because of Your power and Your love, I can have a sound mind and the peace that passes understanding.

I smile. My children laugh now. They are no longer filled with uncertainty when they see me trusting in You. You are our tower of strength, our stronghold. We can shout and sing and praise You for that promise.

ABUNDANT BLESSINGS

O fear the LORD, ye his saints:
for there is no want to them that fear him.

PSALM 34:9

Father, some might think this verse could never be true, but I know different. You, who are truth, would never say something false in Your Word.

The children want more toys than they could possibly play with. I long for many material things—at least temporarily. However, when we are all truly focused on You, the worldly things we want disappear. Then Your desires for us become our desires.

When I see my children sharing with others, dropping their money in the offering plate, and bowing their heads to pray, I know they are learning to reverence You by doing Your will. They are watching me as I do these things. Guide me to always point them to the right example that Jesus set for us.

TWO-PART FORGIVENESS

*Forgive us our debts,
as we forgive our debtors.*

MATTHEW 6:12

Lord, I often forget that forgiveness has two parts. I want to reap all the benefits of Your forgiveness and the forgiveness of others, but I'm not always so eager to grant it.

For instance, I get so tired of the people who believe I should raise my children the exact way they brought up their own families. It's true that some of their advice is good, but some of it is not practical for our family. It wouldn't be so bad, but if I choose not to do something their way, they become critical. It would be easy to harbor anger and resentment, but I know it's wrong.

I need Your help to forgive others as You've forgiven me.

FORGIVE AND PRAY

When ye stand praying, forgive,
if ye have ought against any:
that your Father also which is in heaven
may forgive you your trespasses.

MARK 11:25

Lord, I pray for my children often, and I know I should, but sometimes when I've battled whining and belligerence all day, I need to make sure I've first forgiven them. After all, it does seem rather contradictory to ask for Your blessings on them when my own heart doesn't exactly feel like blessing them.

I guess what I'm asking You to do is to give me a clean heart—one that will have the proper attitude toward my children. That way I'll truly be able to forgive them, and I'll have the right perspective when I pray for them. I do cherish them and want Your blessing on their lives! Please help us all, Father.

TEACHING FORGIVENESS

*Be ye kind one to another, tenderhearted,
forgiving one another,
even as God for Christ's sake
hath forgiven you.*

EPHESIANS 4:32

This is such a popular verse to teach children, Jesus. I think it's one of the first they memorize. But so often it seems that the verse is only used to talk about kindness. The other areas—tenderheartedness and forgiveness—are often overlooked. I know that when children are young it is necessary for us to break things down in order for them to grasp certain truths. I pray that I will never neglect to teach my little ones each concept of Your Word.

I know You will give me plenty of opportunities to help my children understand kindness, tenderheartedness, and—in a home with multiple siblings—forgiveness. I've learned from experience that forgiveness is one of the greatest kindnesses a person can offer.

GIVING UP A GRUDGE

*The discretion of a man deferreth his anger;
and it is his glory to pass over a transgression.*

I think I've discovered how dangerous it is to harbor a grudge. It seems, Lord, that if I don't deal immediately with something that makes me angry I begin to make the situation a lot worse than it already is.

Some days, when everything has gone in the opposite direction of my plans, I begin to have pity parties for myself. I look at everything my children, husband, neighbors, and anyone else have done wrong and magnify it in an attempt to blame someone other than myself and to justify my bad attitude.

But You've told me that I should overlook the faults of others and that I should set aside my anger. Please help me do things Your way, Father.

HEALTHY DESIRES

He will fulfil the desire of them that fear him:
he also will hear their cry,
and will save them.

PSALM 145:19

Father, I feel so unfulfilled. According to the world's standards, I should have a good job, run my house, raise my children—be a Supermom. I don't feel like I'm adequately doing any of those things. Some days I can barely deal with my two-year-old's constant questions. The criticism from neighbors and family weighs heavy on me.

I know I'm looking in the wrong direction for fulfillment. The world doesn't care about me or my needs. Only You can take care of the desires of my heart. Allow me to feel the joy and contentment that come from being filled with You, Lord. Then my children will also see the truth and seek You. When they know You personally, then my heart will be filled to overflowing.

FULFILLING THE LAW

Owe no man any thing,
but to love one another:
for he that loveth another hath fulfilled the law.

ROMANS 13:8

Love one another, Lord? Everyone? No matter what? In the natural, I'm tempted to ask if You understand what You're asking, but I know You do. After all, You loved me before I even knew You—when I still lived for and in the world. How could I ever doubt that You know what You're asking of me?

Just as You have loved me, not based on my actions, I need to love my children, based on Your example. They are gifts from You and worthy of my love, even when their human nature is shining brightly. How many times have I acted like a spoiled two-year-old? Fill me with Your unconditional love, Lord, that I might fulfill the law. May I always love like You love.

ALL GOOD THINGS
COME TO PASS

*Behold, this day I am going the way of all the earth:
and ye know in all your hearts and in all your souls,
that not one thing hath failed of all the good
things which the LORD your God spake
concerning you; all are come to pass unto you,
and not one thing hath failed thereof.*

JOSHUA 23:14

I want to shout, Lord. I want to sing, grab everyone I meet, and tell them about all the wonderful things You have done for me.

Earlier today, I was so discouraged. As a mother, as a Christian, I felt like a failure. Life weighed me down until I couldn't see anything You had accomplished for me. Then I thought of the song "Count Your Blessings." When I started the list, I couldn't stop finding ways You had fulfilled Your promises to me.

The miracle of having children is one of those blessings, Lord. Make me a blessing to my children. I will share my list with them and teach them to count all the good things You've also brought to pass for them.

God's True Promises

God is not a man, that he should lie;
neither the son of man, that he should repent:
hath he said, and shall he not do it?
or hath he spoken,
and shall he not make it good?

Numbers 23:19

One of my children lied to me today, Father. Oh, the pain I felt! I've raised my children to always tell the truth, even when it hurts. Sometimes I've been tempted to lie, but I haven't. I do try to be a good example for them; however, there is always the human nature at work and the influence of the world.

You are not like that, Lord. You are truth; You will never lie. Your example of always being trustworthy is the best one to give my children. Their lives will be made full by the fact that they can trust Your Word in all things.

Take away my anger. Fill me with wisdom and understanding. Speak, Lord. I will listen and be fulfilled.

A HOSPITABLE HOSTESS

*Use hospitality one to another
without grudging.*

1 PETER 4:9

Lord, sometimes I am not generous with my home. It's okay if I've invited someone to my home, but it's the impromptu visits I don't handle very well. It's not that I don't want company, even when it's unexpected. It's just that I'm terrible at thinking on my feet about refreshments. And I'm too self-conscious about the way my house looks. I'm usually too busy playing with my children and their toys to clean up the lunch dishes. Then it's time to make supper and the playthings are left on the floor.

Please help me be a better housekeeper. Even more importantly, Lord, show me how to always have an open welcome—even if my visitors see the mounds of toys and stacks of dishes in the sink.

MEETING NEEDS

The liberal soul shall be made fat:
and he that watereth
shall be watered also himself.

PROVERBS 11:25

Father, there are many people in this world who are needy. Some lack the basic necessities of life, such as food and clothing. Others lack time or friendship. Open my eyes to the needs of others, and guide me to reach out to people as You give me the opportunities.

I try to teach my children to share. What better way is there to do that than to give them an example? And, who knows? Maybe someday it will be me or one of my children who is in need. I would be much more content to receive help from others if I knew that when I'd had the chance I had reached out to them.

Instill in me a generous spirit, Lord.

CONSIDER THE POOR

*Blessed is he that considereth the poor:
the LORD will deliver him in time of trouble.*

PSALM 41:1

God, each year when Christmas comes around, it seems the number of people asking for donations for the poor increases. It even comes into the church.

Being bombarded like that tends to make me cynical. Please help me not to be that way. It's true that I can't give to each cause or person in need. It's also true that not all the cases are legitimate. I need Your wisdom to know what my part should be.

It's not my place to be judgmental either, but sometimes it seems it's the laziness of parents that causes a family to suffer. Help me not to increase a child's suffering by thinking more of the parents' neglect and less of the child's need. After all, I wouldn't want that for my children.

Give me a compassionate heart and discernment in knowing how much to give to others.

GIVE

Give, and it shall be given unto you;
good measure, pressed down,
and shaken together, and running over,
shall men give into your bosom.
For with the same measure that ye mete withal
it shall be measured to you again.

LUKE 6:38

You've made it plenty clear, Lord, that giving is a command—not an option. You've also made it plain what the results of obedience to this command will be. Father, I have so many good opportunities to give. I already know that I'm to give my tithe to the church. I can give beyond that as You speak to my heart and provide the finances.

And I can give more than money. I can find ways to serve in the church or just to spend extra time nurturing my children. Lord, You told me to give and that, if I do, it shall be given to me. You don't say what "it" is, but Your generosity is unmatched and Your blessings are always wonderful! Thank You!

GENTLENESS AND PATIENCE

The servant of the Lord must not strive;
but be gentle unto all men,
apt to teach, patient.

2 TIMOTHY 2:24

Lord, it's abundantly clear that gentleness and patience go together. I am not by nature a patient person, and that leaves the possibility of gentleness in question. If there's one thing children need, it's a gentle mother. They need to be assured by soft words and easy handling. Then, regardless of what they do and no matter what the surrounding circumstances are, they will know they are loved.

Harsh words break down self-confidence and harm a child's feelings of being worthwhile. Oh, help me, Father, not to be responsible for such destruction in the lives of my children. Guide me in how to gently *and* patiently teach them, discipline them, and love them. I want to give my children confidence in who they are and what they can do for You.

Gentle Wisdom

*The wisdom that is from above is first pure,
then peaceable, gentle, and easy to be intreated,
full of mercy and good fruits, without partiality,
and without hypocrisy.*

James 3:17

Lord, I need Your gentle wisdom for every area of life. I'm so thankful that what You offer is the best. Sometimes my own wisdom leads me to deal with my children in ways that aren't exactly gentle.

I don't want to do things my way, Father. I want to be gentle with the precious lives You've entrusted to me and with others, even when I'm tired, frustrated, or confused. I know that I can only do this through the wisdom and power that You offer.

Direct me daily to accept and apply the strength that You've offered so that I will truly have the gentle spirit that You intended me to have. Thank You, Jesus, that I don't have to do this on my own.

TEACHING GENTLENESS

*Put them in mind to be subject
to principalities and powers, to obey magistrates,
to be ready to every good work,
to speak evil of no man, to be no brawlers,
but gentle, shewing all meekness unto all men.*

TITUS 3:1–2

Father, this seems like a long list of principles that I should be teaching my kids, especially when it's added to the many other things Your Word instructs me to instill in their lives. I guess it's not quite as overwhelming, though, when I stop to realize if these principles are present in my life and obvious in my behavior that will be the best instruction I can give to my children. The trick is to make sure that I am applying the principles to my life.

The first half of this list isn't really that tough—maybe because they are not quite so personal. But it becomes a little harder when it concerns my relationship with other people.

Even so, I want to teach my children to be kind and gentle, and I want to be the right example for them. Please show me the way.

61

CHERISHING MY CHILDREN

We were gentle among you,
even as a nurse cherisheth her children.

1 THESSALONIANS 2:7

As I sit here watching my little ones quietly and happily playing with their toys, my heart sings with the love I have for them. I want to pick them up and draw them close. When they're tearing through the house at breakneck speed, I still love them, but catching them for a hug would be difficult. Being gentle when they break something in their haste is also easier said than done.

Father, You gave me my children to cherish, and that includes being gentle with them. I do treasure them, Lord, so help me to impart Your gentleness to them. Help me to draw them close when that's needed and to become involved in their play when that would be better. Mold me into the mother they need.

THE MOST PROFITABLE

Refuse profane and old wives' fables,
and exercise thyself rather unto godliness.
For bodily exercise profiteth little:
but godliness is profitable unto all things,
having promise of the life that now is,
and of that which is to come.

1 TIMOTHY 4:7–8

Lord, this passage is full of wonderful words: *exercise*, *godliness*, *profitable*, and *promise*. I've never been the best at exercising the body, but I want to be faithful at exercising godliness. It's hard work, Lord, and I need reminders to continue with it.

When I get angry or impatient with my children, I'm not exercising godliness, and I know that sometimes I can't seem to help it. Daily pressures build up. Everyday demands take their toll. I ignore my spiritual exercises.

But You promise that "godliness is profitable unto all things." Bodily exercise is good, but I need to exercise my "spiritual muscles" by faithfully practicing godliness. My children will benefit from a mother who isn't impatient with them but who demonstrates godly character. Thank You for assisting me in this.

The Person I Should Be

Seeing then that all these things shall be dissolved,
what manner of persons ought ye to be
in all holy conversation and godliness.

2 Peter 3:11

Lord, forgive me. I've done it again. Sometimes my mouth gets ahead of my brain and I say things I shouldn't say. I yell at the kids or say cutting remarks out of frustration or exhaustion. I don't want to be this way, Lord. How can I ever teach them godliness and gentle conversation when I lose it like this? Please mold me into a more godly woman.

I know this world with all its troubles will one day pass away, so I shouldn't let the little incidents get to me so easily. The spills, the crying, the temper tantrums—a hundred things wear on my nerves. In the midst of it all, Father, give me the peace I need to be a godly woman with holy conversation.

QUIET AUTHORITY

*For kings, and for all that are in authority;
that we may lead a quiet and peaceable life
in all godliness and honesty.*

1 TIMOTHY 2:2

Jesus, I am not a king; nor am I even close to being one or a person who has that sort of power. However, I do have authority over my children. I am the one they look to for leadership when my husband is gone.

I don't feel very peaceable and quiet a lot of the time. My children aren't peaceable and quiet either. Some days they can't seem to settle down and do the chores or studies required of them. Those days godliness seems so unattainable— more of an ideal than the lifestyle it should be. I can even understand why some leaders become harsh and callous toward their people.

Lord, help me to maintain godliness even on difficult days. Assist me in bringing peace to my home.

GIVEN BY DIVINE POWER

*According as his divine power hath given unto us
all things that pertain unto life and godliness,
through the knowledge of him
that hath called us to glory and virtue.*

2 PETER 1:3

Father, I often see my two-year-old, hands on hips, stomping her foot, saying, "Do it myself." I am just like that at times. I want to become a godly woman all on my own. I forget that all good things come from You, Lord, and not from my own efforts.

I need to study Your Word and grow in knowledge of You in order to attain godliness. That is my part. Then I can help my children understand how to live godly lives. You have already given us all the things we need for life and godliness. You are the Great Provider.

I'm called to live a godly life—not by my childishness but by Your grace and virtue. Thank You for Your provision.

KNOWING HOW
TO DO GOD'S WORK

*Study to shew thyself approved unto God,
a workman that needeth not to be ashamed,
rightly dividing the word of truth.*

2 TIMOTHY 2:15

Dear God, a special part of the work You've given me to do on this earth is to bring up my children in a proper way. Sometimes that task seems rather daunting, especially considering the many facets of each child's life. Of course, there are countless parenting books, some of which contain some very helpful information. However, all of that information can be overwhelming. It's hard to distinguish what is good and what is bad.

Father, Your Word contains the best parenting instruction and advice I could ever possess. As I study Your truths, I want to know them so well that I automatically apply them when I care for my children. Give me the wisdom to weigh everything else I read against what the Bible says. Thank You for leading me in right paths.

DAY-LONG MEDITATION

O how love I thy law!
It is my meditation all the day.

PSALM 119:97

Thank You, God, for Your Word. It instructs me how to live. It brings joy to my days and gives strength when I am weak. Each morning Your Spirit guides me to read something that You know I will need throughout the day.

You instruct us to attend to Your Word. As I read it, it is a constant reminder of Your love for me. I cannot doubt that You'll be with me every moment, because it says You will never leave me nor forsake me. It also reminds me of how much You love my kids and that You have their best interests at heart (see Psalm 115:14). I pray that they will love Your Word and understand how special they are to You and that You have something for each of them to meditate on each day.

TAKING GOD AT HIS WORD

As for God, his way is perfect;
the word of the LORD is tried:
he is a buckler to all them that trust in him.

2 SAMUEL 22:31

Father, I've discovered that in order for me to have a close relationship with You I have to completely trust You and take You at Your Word. Too often I only partly trust You.

For example, when You say in 2 Corinthians 12:9, "My grace is sufficient for thee: for my strength is made perfect in weakness," my mind screams out, *I don't understand! The baby's teething and crying all night. My toddler refuses to stay in bed, and the dog won't quit barking. I'm exhausted, and I don't understand how any good can come of this.*

I'm ashamed to admit, Lord, that sometimes I have a hard time taking You at Your Word. Please show me how to trust You more, even when my mind can't grasp it and my heart can't accept it.

Pointing out the Truth

The word of God is quick, and powerful,
and sharper than any two-edged sword,
piercing even to the dividing
asunder of soul and spirit,
and of the joints and marrow,
and is a discerner of the thoughts
and intents of the heart.

Hebrews 4:12

Sometimes the truth hurts, Lord. I know Your Word is always honest and will point out the shortcomings in my life. It will tell me when my temper is out of line or when my priorities are wrong. It will show me when I've dealt with my children in an ungodly way.

I'm no different than anyone else. I don't like to see my wrongdoings, but I know that through Your Word and the Holy Spirit You point these things out for my own good. You want me to do better, so You let me know when I'm wrong. That way I can come to You for cleansing and an opportunity to make things right. Thank You for the truth in Your Word, even though sometimes the truth hurts.

GREEN PASTURES

He maketh me to lie down in green pastures:
he leadeth me beside the still waters.

PSALM 23:2

Green pastures. Oh, how I love the smell of the grass, the feel of it under my bare feet, and the sight of the jewel-like color. I should want to lie down in the softness and relax—to revel in Your leading.

The problem is I don't always want to lie down and rest in the pasture that You have provided. Sometimes my "pastures" seem dry. The grass feels brown and withered. I look at my house, and then I see the neighbor's house; it doesn't need a coat of paint. Their children seem better behaved. Sometimes I long to leave the place You have for me.

Thank You for making me to lie down even when I don't want to. Thank You for leading me beside quiet waters when I need the solace.

Walking in the Way

*Thine ears shall hear a word behind thee,
saying, This is the way, walk ye in it,
when ye turn to the right hand,
and when ye turn to the left.*

Isaiah 30:21

Why is it, Lord, that I know You are guiding me, yet I don't seem to know the way? I get caught up in the cares of the world. The children are demanding attention. There's laundry to do, lunches to fix, cleaning that can't wait. Something always calls louder than the voice You're speaking in, yet You are the one I need to listen to the most.

I get discouraged when I don't know which way to go—where You're leading me. Perhaps the problem is that I'm not taking the time to truly hear what You're saying. You are right behind me, Lord, telling me which way to turn. I want to be quiet and listen for Your guidance.

A MORE WONDERFUL PLACE

This God is our God for ever and ever:
he will be our guide even unto death.

PSALM 48:14

My heart is breaking, Lord. The death of someone we love is one of the hardest things to cope with. I know the loved one is in heaven, but I selfishly want that person to still be here with me. I can gain comfort from reading Psalm 116:15. Help me to rejoice instead of feeling sorry for myself.

I know the children are watching my reactions. I can see it in their eyes—in their solemn attitude. Their reactions now, and as adults, hinge so much on the way I react to the trials I face. Please show me the way to set a good example.

Fill me with the joy that comes from knowing You are my God forever and ever. You won't desert me. When death does come, You will be there to guide me to a place more wonderful than I can ever imagine.

THE SPIRIT OF TRUTH

Howbeit when he, the Spirit of truth, is come,
he will guide you into all truth:
for he shall not speak of himself;
but whatsoever he shall hear,
that shall he speak:
and he will shew you things to come.

JOHN 16:13

Shh. Quiet. Your Spirit often speaks in a still, small voice. I'm so busy yelling over the cacophony, answering phones, or running the vacuum that I don't hear You, Lord. Only when I slow down and listen do I hear.

I'll gather the children with me, Father. We can kneel together, learn to have a time of stillness, a time for You to speak. As we're gathered together, speak to us, Lord. Show us the truths we need to know. Help us to trust You for the truths yet to come.

Your guidance is trustworthy. You are our Good Shepherd. You lead us to places of rest when we need them. My children and I need that rest. Thank You for Your leading.

JOY IN EVERY TASK

*Thou shalt rejoice before the LORD thy God
in all that thou puttest thine hands unto.*

DEUTERONOMY 12:18

There's no mistaking here, Lord—You've made
it clear that I'm to be joyful in each and every task.
This includes the things I enjoy, like baking cook-
ies for my family, as well as the seemingly endless
tasks of washing and folding laundry.

If I look at these chores with a proper attitude, I am reminded that each one truly is a blessing. You've given me my wonderful husband and
beautiful children who make all this work necessary. You've also given me the strength and ability
to accomplish these tasks.

The next time I'm tempted to complain about
the mounds of work, remind me to turn the murmuring into praise. I am a blessed woman indeed.

Rejoice in the Lord

I will be glad and rejoice in thee:
I will sing praise to thy name,
O thou most High.

Psalm 9:2

O thou most High! When I put into perspective that You truly are the most high God, how can I help but rejoice in You? It is only because of You that I live and breathe. It is because of Your love that I was placed into a family who loves me deeply. It is Your goodness that has given me my own husband and children to nurture. And it's Your marvelous grace that took me into Your arms and made me Your child.

Father, praising You and rejoicing in You must be high on my priority list. Proclaiming Your love to others must never be lacking in my life. Thank You that I am able to rejoice in You!

ETERNAL JOY

Well done, thou good and faithful servant:
thou hast been faithful over a few things,
I will make thee ruler over many things:
enter thou into the joy of thy Lord.

MATTHEW 25:21

Father, this parable is such a clear picture of faithfulness to You and the joy that results from that faithfulness. Like the servant in this story, You've given me work to do. First, I am called to live my life in the way that all Christians are commanded to live.

My work also includes being a godly wife and bringing up my children according to Your Word. I should do everything I do in a way that gives honor and glory to You.

The promised result—eternal joy—brings a great amount of anticipation to my heart. What is even more exciting is that if I am faithful in these tasks You will trust me with others. Then there will be even more of Your joy to experience.

FULL OF JOY

Thou hast made known to me the ways of life;
thou shalt make me full of joy
with thy countenance.

ACTS 2:28

The ways of life encompass so much, dear Jesus. One of the ways of life that You've given me is motherhood. There's so much joy included in that. Simply watching each new achievement thrills me. Seeing my daughter toddle across the floor—a newly acquired accomplishment for her—reminds me that You are in charge of even those natural skills in life. You will give the ability when the time is right.

Joy fills my life when my son asks to have a book read, then chooses one about You. You know his favorite song is "Away in a Manger." I pray that this is the beginning of a close walk that he will eventually have with You. That will bring the greatest amount of joy, not only to him but also to his mother.

REACHING OUT

*I watch, and am as a sparrow
alone upon the house top.*

PSALM 102:7

Another day has passed when all I hear are the voices of children. I know I should be happy with that, but I need someone to talk to who doesn't need his or her face washed or shoes tied.

I love my children, Lord. I thank You for them, but sometimes I need another person to talk to who understands what I'm going through. I feel so isolated, so cut off from the rest of the world.

Help me reach out to another woman—maybe one of the mothers from church or my neighborhood who needs the kind of companionship I do. Give me the willingness to reach out to that person—to get my focus off myself. Give me rest, knowing You will be there.

Feeling Forsaken

*Zion said, The LORD hath forsaken me,
and my Lord hath forgotten me.*

Isaiah 49:14

There are times, Lord, when I feel as if You've forgotten me. I don't feel Your presence. I can't see Your guidance. It's like walking alone in the dark.

Yet, Lord, this passage goes on to say that though a mother might forsake her child You will never forget me. I am engraved on the palms of Your hands. The Creator of the entire universe holds me in His hands! How could I let those feelings of being forsaken overwhelm me?

Forgive me, Lord, for those times when I've doubted Your love. Let me close my eyes, hold out my hand, and know that You are there. You are leading me and loving me, no matter what my emotions say. Thank You for being with me, Father.

ALONE, YET NOT ALONE

Behold, the hour cometh, yea,
is now come, that ye shall be scattered,
every man to his own, and shall leave me alone:
and yet I am not alone,
because the Father is with me.

JOHN 16:32

My child is so alone, Lord. Something happened. All her friends have deserted her. I ache at the hurt and anguish I see reflected in her face. I want to make it all go away—to erase this incident.

We talked about how You were abandoned by everyone when You faced the cross, Jesus. Your darkest hour, the time You needed Your friends the most, yet they left You. Even so, You weren't alone. The Father was there with You, a comfort to You.

I see my daughter gleaning solace from this passage. The loneliness will pass. Her friends will return. Most of all, she's learned that You are always beside her. This is a lesson she won't soon forget. Thank You, Jesus, for being the perfect example.

Caring for My Soul

I looked on my right hand, and beheld,
but there was no man that would know me:
refuge failed me; no man cared for my soul.

Psalm 142:4

Here I am, Lord, in the midst of a crowd, yet I feel so alone. I don't know anyone; no one knows me. Does anyone here even care that I'm hurting inside? I feel as if there is no safe place anywhere for me.

Is this the way my children felt when I sent them off to school for the first time or to church camp, where they didn't know anyone? Were they lonely in the midst of a crowd?

Sometimes the Christian walk can be draining. I think of Elijah and how discouraged he became. He thought he was alone too, but You showed him he wasn't. Lord, You care for our souls, for every part of us. You are there to keep us from being alone.

Active Love

My little children,
let us not love in word, neither in tongue;
but in deed and in truth.

1 John 3:18

Lord, I'm always telling people how much I love my children, but I'm afraid I'm not always good at putting it into practice. In my heart I know I do love them and want what's best for them, but I often get so caught up in what needs to be done that I forget to show my children how important they actually are.

Father, let Your love fill my heart so that it pours over and floods the children You've so graciously given me. Let me show them how special they are to me. Let them understand the depth of Your love because they see it exemplified in me. Help my words of love to take on new meaning as they are backed by my actions to prove it.

Loving God

The LORD preserveth all them that love him:
but all the wicked will he destroy.

PSALM 145:20

I know it's important for me to love my family as
well as other people, but it's even more important
that I love You, Lord. Of course, I realize that if I
truly love You the way that I'm supposed to all
other aspects of my life, including love for others,
will fall into place.

Thank You for Your promise to preserve me if
I love You, Father. I know that this is an eternal
promise. What more incentive do I need to pur-
sue a right walk with You? Besides, I also understand that Your promise to destroy the wicked is
equally eternal. How much better it is to love You
and to spend eternity with You than to be wicked
and eternally destroyed!

Keep me in the right path, Lord.

SACRIFICIAL LOVE

*Walk in love, as Christ also hath loved us,
and hath given himself for us an offering
and a sacrifice to God
for a sweetsmelling savour.*

EPHESIANS 5:2

Thank You, Jesus, for Your sacrificial love for me. Thank You also for the example of true love that You have provided.

Lord, true love often requires giving of one's self. I'm learning where that might be true in parenting. Having children has brought about many changes in my life. They've all been worthwhile, but that doesn't mean they've all been easy. A certain amount of freedom had to be surrendered. My schedule had to be renovated in order to meet the demands of my children. Even basic tasks like grocery shopping have a new level of difficulty. But these changes are so worthwhile when I look at the happy smiles on my children's faces or feel their little arms around my neck. Love is beautiful!

EASIER SAID THAN DONE

Let all your things be done with charity.

1 CORINTHIANS 16:14

Father, You've commanded me to do everything with charity, or love. That's hard. I mean, I love my kids, and I want to show them my love each moment; but when it's 2:30 a.m. and one of them is already up for the fourth time, frustration creeps in, and love goes into hiding.

Sometimes I know my child is not tired enough and needs a loving disciplinary reminder that he must stay in bed even if he doesn't want to. Other times he doesn't feel well, or he's afraid of a storm. Remind me, Lord, of the times that I could have used a comforting hug.

Help me to put my need for sleep aside, to draw my child close, and to assure him of my love and, more importantly, of Your love.

UNDERSTANDING MEEKNESS

The LORD lifteth up the meek:
he casteth the wicked down to the ground.

PSALM 147:6

Lord, You've offered a wonderful reward for meekness; but, to be honest, I'm not sure I fully understand meekness. It seems to encompass so many other character traits—graciousness, love, gentleness, patience. I've always heard that meekness isn't weakness; it's strength under control. All of these traits seem to fit into the category of gentle strength.

I suppose that meekness is really the kind of strength I need as a mother, so I can be strong enough to discipline with love and firmness. If I display gentle strength, I can help my children as they face sorrow and disappointment. I do not want a cruel strength that frightens or intimidates my children. Show me, Lord, how to understand meekness and to have this controlled strength.

A SERVANT'S HEART

*Blessed are the meek:
for they shall inherit the earth.*

MATTHEW 5:5

You know, at first this looks like an inheritance I might not really want. The way the earth is today doesn't make the offer very attractive, but I understand that this promise is for those who will inherit the earth with You, Jesus, when You set up Your kingdom here. You don't want someone involved in Your inheritance who thinks that she has to be in charge all the time. You want someone full of meekness—someone with a servant's heart.

Sometimes, as a mother, I need a reminder that what I should be is a servant. I get so wrapped up in the need to maintain order, which is important, that I forget my job: to meet the needs of my family. Please give me a servant's heart.

WORTHY OF MY CALLING

I therefore, the prisoner of the Lord,
beseech you that ye walk worthy of
the vocation wherewith ye are called,
with all lowliness and meekness,
with longsuffering, forbearing one another in love.

EPHESIANS 4:1–2

Father, I believe that many people don't understand that the call to motherhood comes from You. They might not understand how much work goes into this vocation. At times it's hard for me—and other mothers, I'm sure—because some people expect us to drop what we're doing to meet their wants or needs.

I want to scream, "Hey, taking care of my kids is a time-consuming and exhausting business." I either want to feel sorry for myself or pat myself on the back for dedicating my life to motherhood. But, Lord, I know that both attitudes are improper.

I should approach my calling with a meek and humble spirit. Only when my outlook becomes Christlike will I truly be considered worthy of this calling.

A PROMISE TO THE MEEK

The meek will he guide in judgment:
and the meek will he teach his way.

PSALM 25:9

Dear God, I have a lot of questions about life, children, and my role as a mother. This Scripture gives a beautiful promise for me as long as I am meek. You've said that You would guide and direct me.

The thing is, Father, I sometimes have trouble with meekness. I speak when I should remain silent. I get involved in business not belonging to me. I do other things that don't fit into the category of meekness.

Please forgive me, Jesus. First of all, I want to be meek because my desire is to be like You. Also, I really need the guidance You will give me. I want to please You in all I say and do. Help me to depend on You instead of on myself.

A MOTHER'S COMFORT

*As one whom his mother comforteth,
so will I comfort you;
and ye shall be comforted in Jerusalem.*

ISAIAH 66:13

Lord, You've allowed a mother's comfort to be a beautiful illustration of the comfort You extend to Your children. My desire is to live up to this picture.

I can't begin to count the number of times You've wrapped Your loving arms around me and calmed me in the midst of fears. You've drawn me near in times of sorrow, and You've given me assurance when I've faced great disappointment.

Dear Jesus, I want to do the same for my children. In this world it is certain that there will be many opportunities to offer comfort to my little ones. Help me to always be there for them to comfort them as You comfort me.

MY FAMILY'S FUTURE

*The children ought not to lay up for the parents,
but the parents for the children.*

2 CORINTHIANS 12:14

Father, I know that Paul is talking about a spiritual family in this passage, but as I read it, I find I can make application to my own family. It concerns me, because as I look at families in general, I see a trend that doesn't seem to go along with Your Word. Children reach adulthood, and parents quit parenting. Do parents really believe there's no more they should do once their children become adults?

Direct me in how to be involved in the lives of my children. While they're young, I want to instill in them the basics of Your Word and show them how to apply the Word in their everyday lives. Then, as they mature, help me build on those teachings by setting the right example, praying for them, being there for them, and caring for them.

FAMILY FAITH

I call to remembrance the
unfeigned faith that is in thee,
which dwelt first in thy grandmother Lois,
and thy mother Eunice;
and I am persuaded that in thee also.

2 TIMOTHY 1:5

What a challenge this is, Father! Timothy was a man full of faith, and that faith started with his grandmother, who passed it on to his mother, who passed it on to him. Because of his faith, Timothy was able to accomplish great things for You.

I want my children to serve You too, but I know they can only do that if they have true faith in You. Guide me so that I can be the example to them that Eunice was to Timothy. When the time comes, let me be an example to my grandchildren as well.

What greater task could I have than to make sure my children are introduced to You? Help me live so that they will want this kind of faith.

Teachable Moments

Ye shall teach them your children,
speaking of them when
thou sittest in thine house,
and when thou walkest by the way,
when thou liest down,
and when thou risest up.

Deuteronomy 11:19

Dear Jesus, most of the mothers I know are always on the lookout for teachable moments that are age appropriate for their children. I'm no different. I want my kids to learn the alphabet, numbers, and shapes, and to learn to feed and dress themselves. I look for opportunities to make these learning experiences fun and effective.

You've pointed out that, as a mother, I need to take advantage of the teachable moments You give me to teach my children the truths of Your Word. You give me opportunities each day. I pray that I'll never let one pass by. I know that these teaching moments will have lasting value in their lives.

KEEPING GOD'S COMMANDMENTS

Let us hear the conclusion of the whole matter:
Fear God, and keep his commandments:
for this is the whole duty of man.

ECCLESIASTES 12:13

Father, what counts in this life is that I have a great reverence for You and that I obey Your commands. If I do this, I won't go wrong, and that includes being a good mother to my children. You've given me plenty of instruction on parenting, and it's because You know what's best. Thank You for seeing the need to include parenting in Your Word.

Your law is packed full of other areas that aren't specific to parenting but can and should certainly be included. After all, You've told us that if we break Your law in part, we've broken it in full.

Help me, Lord, to fear and obey You in *all* areas of life, for that is indeed my whole duty.

Reward of Obedience

*In thy seed shall all the nations
of the earth be blessed;
because thou hast obeyed my voice.*

Genesis 22:18

Dear God, I have found that obeying You is a very satisfying experience, even by itself. But the reward for obedience goes far beyond that; it affects many more people. You told Abraham that because of his obedience You'd bless the whole earth through his seed.

I know that You won't use my children in the same way You used Abraham's, but I know that they can still be blessings to many people.

I want to obey You in everything and also lead my children to obey You. Through our obedience to You, help us to reach many people for Your kingdom. That truly is the greatest blessing. I'm thankful that obedience is so rewarding!

TEACHING OBEDIENCE

Children, obey your parents in the Lord:
for this is right. Honour thy father and mother;
which is the first commandment with promise;
that it may be well with thee,
and thou mayest live long on the earth.

EPHESIANS 6:1–3

I think that maybe this is every parent's favorite Scripture, Lord. We all want these to become our children's life verses. The funny thing is that we seem to just expect it to happen. We fail to realize that we need to have an active part in this obedience.

I want my children to know what I expect of them and then obey. Give me guidance to establish the right reward and discipline system. Probably the hardest, yet most important, aspect of this education is my own consistency. I need strength in that area, Lord.

I also need to show them how important obedience is by being obedient myself—to You and to others in authority over me. Thank You for assisting me in this effort.

A DESIRE TO OBEY

Behold, I have longed after thy precepts:
quicken me in thy righteousness.
So shall I keep thy law
continually for ever and ever.

PSALM 119:40, 44

Lord, my intentions to obey are good. I mean, I've read Your Word, and I know what it says You expect of me. I want to obey all Your commands but, honestly, I'm weak. So many times I fail because I am relying on my own strength and righteousness. Please give me Your righteousness, Jesus. When I have Your power, I will be able to follow Your commands.

Sometimes I look at the faces of my children when they're contemplating actions to take. They know and understand what I expect of them, but the desire to do their own thing overwhelms them.

I want to help them do what's right, and I'm depending on You to show me how. Make us all more willing to accept the assistance that's offered.

AFFLICTION

*Rejoicing in hope; patient in tribulation;
continuing instant in prayer.*

ROMANS 12:12

I'm trying to be joyful in the hope I have in You, and I've been faithful in prayer, Lord. It's the having patience in affliction that is hard. When I hurt, I want the pain to stop immediately—not after I've learned the lesson I need to learn.

I don't mean to snap at the children. Their enthusiasm for life sometimes becomes an irritant to me. Even their accidents make me grit my teeth to keep from screaming. That shouldn't happen, but it does.

As I learn to rest in You, Lord, renew me. Give me the ability I need to be patient, no matter what trouble is around me. Let my joyful hope and my faithful prayers build up my patience.

RESTING IN THE LORD

Rest in the LORD, and wait patiently for him:
fret not thyself because of him
who prospereth in his way,
because of the man who
bringeth wicked devices to pass.

PSALM 37:7

Sometimes I want to shout in anger at the un-
fairness of life, Lord. I see on the news how many
of the prosperous people get away with all sorts of
crime. If I were to do the same, I would receive
severe punishment. How can they seem to get
away with everything?

Then I use that to teach my children. I tell
them that, even though there may be times when
these people think they've gotten away with some
wrong, You are watching, and they will have to
answer for their sins eventually. We all will, Lord.

Help me to not judge but to let You decide
the fairness of matters. Give me patience—to rest
in You and to wait for Your return. I need Your
help to teach my children to rest in You too.

HAPPINESS
THROUGH ENDURANCE

Behold, we count them happy which endure.
Ye have heard of the patience of Job,
and have seen the end of the Lord;
that the Lord is very pitiful,
and of tender mercy.

JAMES 5:11

Whine. Whine. Whine. That's all I seem to do, Lord. I'm sure You get tired of me never being satisfied. When things are going well, I complain about not growing spiritually. When things are going wrong, I complain about the trial. How can You still love me when I'm so weak and impatient to be more like You?

Today I was unpleasant with the children. They were whining because they all wanted their own way. I saw myself reflected in them. Then I thought of the prophets and realized how my troubles are nothing compared to theirs.

Still my complaining heart, Lord. Fill me with rejoicing. You are refining me. I want to teach my children patience by my own example. Give me strength for the task.

HE HEARS MY CRY

I waited patiently for the LORD;
and he inclined unto me,
and heard my cry.

PSALM 40:1

What a rich promise is in this verse, Lord! If I wait patiently, You will listen and hear my cry. Psalm 40:2 talks about being in miry clay. How many times have my troubles dragged me down like clinging clay, yet You were there to rescue me!

Put a new song in my mouth, Lord. Let my children see me being patient and waiting on You, no matter what difficulty I'm facing. Help them learn the same song of joy that You are giving me. Together we can sing Your praises to all those around us. You hear us, Lord. You are our mighty Savior.

When I learn to be patient and trust in You, I know that You will hear my cries and I will be blessed. Thank You for this blessing.

NOTHING IS IMPOSSIBLE

Jesus beheld them,
and said unto them,
With men this is impossible;
but with God all things are possible.

MATTHEW 19:26

I can't imagine it, Lord. I cannot begin to comprehend Your power and ability. I see the impossibility of a situation and forget that You are the God of the possible. Why do I doubt? Why do I tremble in fear when all I really need to do is to turn to You? I picture one of my children holding out a hand to me and know that's what I need to do with You: I need to have childlike trust.

When I see how You have interceded on my behalf, I want to fall on my face before You. My prayers have been answered in miraculous ways. In times when all I could see was darkness, You provided light and power and hope. Thank You, Lord.

PERFECT IN WEAKNESS

He said unto me, My grace is sufficient for thee:
for my strength is made perfect in weakness.
Most gladly therefore will I
rather glory in my infirmities,
that the power of Christ may rest upon me.

2 CORINTHIANS 12:9

Today when I overheard others making fun of my child, I was angry and wanted to speak up. I wanted to inflict punishment and defend my child, who is the weaker one. I thought of all the times when I've been put down and how it hurt me.

Lord, You are made strong in our weaknesses. I need to remember that and teach my children that we should count it all joy when we are faced with trials and suffering. That isn't an easy lesson to learn, Father. It is the opposite from what the world teaches.

I sometimes want to rely on my power rather than Yours, Lord. I pray that my children will witness that Your grace is always sufficient. When we are weak, then we will be strong in You.

INNER POWER

Unto him that is able to do exceeding abundantly above all that we ask or think, according to the power that worketh in us.

EPHESIANS 3:20

This is unbelievable, Lord! I asked You for one simple thing, and You gave me far more than I ever expected. This verse tells me that You do this because of the power working within me.

You are the one at work in me; Your Spirit is a part of me, and He guides my thoughts and actions. Thank You for that. I don't know what I would do if I had to live life on my own.

Not only does Your inner power affect me, I can see it at work in my children as they grow in You, Lord. Your Spirit inside us is a life-changing power that will always be available to us wherever we are. Thank You for this wonderful gift.

FAULTLESS PRESENTATION

*Unto him that is able to keep you from falling,
and to present you faultless before the presence
of his glory with exceeding joy.*

JUDE 24

Faultless? Me, Jesus? Me, the mother who has made so many mistakes while raising her children? How can this be? What amazing power could do this?

Yet, this verse says that You are able to keep me from falling. I look back at the mistakes I've made, and I see the evidence of Your power to change me. I've been growing into a better mother through Your guidance, Lord.

Someday You will present me faultless, cleansed by Your blood. What joy there will be then, Lord—all my sins taken away, no memory of my weaknesses. The evidence of Your power to lift me up and make me whole fills me with exceeding joy. I praise You forever and forever.

THE FRUIT OF OUR LIPS

*By him therefore let us offer the sacrifice
of praise to God continually, that is,
the fruit of our lips giving thanks to his name.*

HEBREWS 13:15

O Father, what have I done? Today in my anger, I said something I shouldn't have. At the time I felt justified, but now I know better.

Your Word says in James 3:10 that blessing and cursing should not come out of the same mouth. How can I praise You in front of my children after they heard my angry words earlier today? Forgive me, Lord. I've asked my children to forgive me too. Give me the courage to apologize to those I wronged.

Make my praise a sacrifice to You, Jesus. Instead of speaking in anger or frustration, I want to fill my mouth with words of continual praise to You. I pray that everything I say will glorify You, Lord.

WITH UTTER JOY

O Lord, open thou my lips;
and my mouth shall shew forth thy praise.

PSALM 51:15

I praise You, Lord. You made the ultimate sacrifice for me so I could know salvation. My heart is overflowing. I want to run out and tell everyone how awesome You are. You alone are able to save the sinful. The Bible says in Romans 3:23 that we are all sinners and need You.

Because of Your sacrifice, Jesus, I want to give something back. You don't want sacrifices like in Old Testament days. What You want is a broken and contrite heart, a spirit that is malleable in Your hands.

Lord, break my heart. Make me a living sacrifice for You that I might lead my children and others to You. Let my praises be a godly example in my home. I praise You with all that is within me.

CALLED INTO THE LIGHT

Ye are a chosen generation,
a royal priesthood, an holy nation,
a peculiar people;
that ye should shew forth the praises
of him who hath called you out of darkness
into his marvelous light.

1 PETER 2:9

Lord, I can't believe it. Scripture says that You chose me from the foundation of the world. From the beginning of time You knew I would one day belong to You. It's too much for me to comprehend. You, the God of all creation, chose me to be made holy through the blood of Your Son, Jesus. You set me apart, Lord.

My praises are so inadequate to express what I feel for You, for the mighty and wondrous thing You've done for me. I probably will never understand what You saw in me.

To You, Lord, I am precious. To me, You are beyond words. I praise You, Lord, with all my being.

Telling Everyone

Sing praises to the Lord,
which dwelleth in Zion:
declare among the people his doings.

Psalm 9:11

Were You blessed today, Lord, at the way my children were praising You before others? My heart was full to bursting as I watched them. As we moved through the store, they were singing of Your love and grace. Everyone we passed heard the witness of these youngsters. Yet, they weren't doing it for their own benefit; they were just praising You because they love You.

How often I become afraid when I know I should talk to others about You. Your Word says we should come to You as a little child. I hope to get my eyes off myself and praise You because of who You are. I want to follow the example of my children.

Thank You for this valuable lesson, Lord.

GOD IS ALWAYS AVAILABLE

Evening, and morning, and at noon,
will I pray, and cry aloud:
and he shall hear my voice.

PSALM 55:17

Thank You, Father, that You are never too busy for me. That's hard for me to fathom, because so often I hear myself saying to my kids, "Just give me a minute. I have to get this done." And it's true, Lord. I really can't be totally available to all of my children every minute of every day.

But, Lord, You are always willing to hear my petitions no matter what the time of day. It doesn't matter if multitudes of other people are bringing requests before You at the same instant. You are God, and You will hear and answer each of us.

Remind me that You really do want me to come before You all day long. And please help me to be more available to my own children.

A Bold Approach

*Let us therefore come boldly
unto the throne of grace,
that we may obtain mercy,
and find grace to help in time of need.*

Hebrews 4:16

So many times, Father, when I need something from someone here on earth, I'm either afraid or embarrassed to ask for it. You've assured me that I don't need to worry about that with You. You knew that I would need You often, so You made a way for me to come to You without fear and at any time. I'm so thankful for that.

It seems that ever since my children were born, I've needed You so much more often. I have so many questions or concerns, and many times I just want to thank You for them.

I'm glad none of this sounds foolish to You. It's wonderful that You will take time for me.

INTERCESSORY PRAYER

Likewise the Spirit also helpeth our infirmities:
for we know not what
we should pray for as we ought:
but the Spirit itself maketh intercession for us
with groanings which cannot be uttered.

ROMANS 8:26

One of the greatest gifts You've given me is the Holy Spirit to intercede for me during prayer. You know, Lord, how many times I've tried to pray and have had to stop and say, "Holy Spirit, I need You to take over for me." Sometimes I'm so confused concerning the matter I'm praying about, and I just don't know how to articulate the request.

Other times it's fear that prevents me from putting words to my prayers. I know that's been especially true as I've tried to completely give my children over to You; I wanted to hoard and care for them myself. Occasionally I try to pray and just get stuck.

Thank You, Holy Spirit, for intervening and making my requests better than I ever could.

I Prayed for a Child

*For this child I prayed;
and the LORD hath given me my petition
which I asked of him.*

1 Samuel 1:27

Thank You for granting my request and blessing me with a beautiful family. Lord, as Hannah did, I give my children back to You. My prayer now is that each of my children would accept You as their personal Savior. Then I ask that You would use each one for Your glory.

Help my children to dedicate themselves to serving You in whatever capacity You would call them. Be with them as they face the many temptations that abound. Show them what convictions to establish and give them the strength to stand firm in those convictions. Please protect them from spiritual and physical harm, and give them sound minds and bodies.

I thank You in advance for answered prayers.

PRIDEFUL PLANS

I say, through the grace given unto me,
to every man that is among you,
not to think of himself more highly
than he ought to think;
but to think soberly, according as God
hath dealt to every man the measure of faith.

ROMANS 12:3

I remember, Father, back when I first considered starting a family. I thought I would be a perfect parent. I knew I'd have some sacrifices to make, but I was sure that would be easy, because I would love my kids completely. I expected to be consistent, so that my children would be perfect angels wherever they went. On top of that, I planned to be the prime example of a loving wife.

It was easier dreamed than done. In all of my prideful planning, I forgot that it takes more than my own self-will to do all these things so well— especially when a lot of things in "perfect" parenting are contrary to my nature. Forgive me, Father, for not turning to You to begin with. I definitely need Your assistance if I'm going to be a good, but not prideful, mother.

PRIDE VERSUS HUMILITY

When pride cometh,
then cometh shame:
but with the lowly is wisdom.

PROVERBS 11:2

Dear Jesus, on the surface, being lowly sounds rather undesirable. But in this case, lowliness accompanies wisdom, and that sounds much better. Pride seems more natural, but when I see that it is coupled with shame, I'd rather not have it.

Father, I know You blessed me abundantly in the children You have given me. Help me not to flaunt them or to take the credit that belongs to You. Remind me to acknowledge that all I am and all they are is because of Your grace. I am proud of my children, Lord, but I don't want this pride to be wicked or foolish; rather, let it be the motherly type that is based on unconditional love.

DON'T FALL

Wherefore let him that thinketh
he standeth take heed lest he fall.

1 CORINTHIANS 10:12

God, You've given us plenty of warnings about the dangers of pride, but it seems we pay so little attention to them. I know that for myself this is often true. Some days I'll start thinking that I've really arrived. I've met so many of my goals, and I'm a fairly strong woman. My kids are the best, and life is great. I begin to take credit for things when I should be glorifying You. About the time that starts happening, I crash.

Father, I should have learned my lesson by now, but even in that area, I'm too proud. Falling hurts, and I don't like it. And I don't like letting pride control me. Please forgive me, and help me get rid of the pride in my life.

LET GOD LIFT YOU UP

*Humble yourselves in the sight of the Lord,
and he shall lift you up.*

JAMES 4:10

Lord Jesus, in this world, honor and reward play too big a part in our lives. We do things to look good in the eyes of other people. We gloat when we are praised. Of course, to some extent working toward this praise is a good motivational tool, but there's a danger in the focus being misplaced.

I know it's so much more important to be pleasing to You. You've given me many wonderful tasks, and being a mother is one of my favorites. However, it also can be very humbling at times. I guess that's good for me, though.

Help me to do the job humbly and to rely on You. That is what would please You most, and that reward is the best motivator I could ask for.

ANGELS WATCHING OVER US

*The angel of the LORD encampeth
round about them that fear him,
and delivereth them.*

PSALM 34:7

Your promise gives me a secure feeling, Lord. I'm surrounded by Your love and protection. I picture the times my children are afraid. I hold them in my arms, tight against me, and whisper words of comfort. They snuggle in close. Their trembling ceases. They relax as their fears fade away. My heart overflows with love as I realize that You love me in the same way.

How many times have I been afraid, yet You sent angels to watch over me? You were my comfort and protector. I can't begin to count the times.

Because You surround me and care for me, I can do the same for my children. Someday my children will do the same for my grandchildren. What a blessed heritage! Thank you for the peace this brings.

FOR EVER AND EVER

As the mountains are round about Jerusalem,
so the LORD is round about his people
from henceforth even for ever.

PSALM 125:2

This morning, Lord, we looked out the windows at the mountains surrounding our little valley. We talked about how permanent the mountains are: They don't fade away or wash away. I explained to the children that You are even more lasting than the mountains and that You surround us in the same way for our protection.

I remember the times when I've held my children close, shielding them from harm or danger. Then I rejoice that You are our protective shield.

As long as we trust in Your presence, we have nothing to worry about. You will be with us forever and ever without end. Nothing can separate us from You, because You are the strong protector, the mighty One who watches over us always. I praise You, Lord, for Your protection.

WITH A HEART FOR GOD

*The eyes of the LORD run to and fro
throughout the whole earth,
to shew himself strong in the behalf of them
whose heart is perfect toward him.*

2 CHRONICLES 16:9

Lord, how can my heart be perfect toward You? On my own I am nothing. Only through You am I complete, made whole. Direct my steps, Father.

This verse tells me You are watching. You know the times I sin. I cover it well most of the time. But, at home, in front of my children—these are some of my worst times. It saddens me, Lord, when I don't set a good example for them.

Make my heart perfect. Take my hand, and give me strength. Be strong for me when I don't measure up. My way to attain a perfect heart is through You, Lord, so don't take Your eyes off me. More than anywhere else, I want a heart for You in my home.

STONES OF A CROWN

The LORD their God shall save them
in that day as the flock of his people:
for they shall be as the stones of a crown,
lifted up as an ensign upon his land.

ZECHARIAH 9:16

Sometimes I get scared, Lord. I worry that I won't be ready when Your trumpet sounds. I'm afraid my children won't be walking right with You. I tremble in fear at the thought of being separated from You.

This verse is a comfort, Father. You are the author of my salvation. All I have to do is turn to You, and You will do the rest. I can place my children in Your hands because You are all-sufficient. You will protect them, because You love them even more than I do.

Cleanse me of my ungrounded fears. Fill me with confidence that I can share with my children. You are the strong protector. I am thankful that, because of Jesus, we will be lifted up as the stones in a crown.

ALWAYS A PURE HEART

The way of man is froward and strange:
but as for the pure, his work is right.

PROVERBS 21:8

Lord, I want to have pure thoughts and a pure heart. Only with You is this possible. On my own I'm full of wickedness. This is not what I want my children to see; I want them to see a mother who has a heart and mind like Jesus.

Some days, when I feel like I'm experiencing a spiritual high, it's easy to think pure and upright thoughts and to walk in Your ways. On days when I'm having spiritual struggles, my thoughts become full of discouragement and frustration, and that invades my actions and attitudes.

I don't like to be so controlled by emotions, Father. Please give me the strength to be pure in every situation.

KEEP THYSELF PURE

Lay hands suddenly on no man,
neither be partaker of other men's sins:
keep thyself pure.

1 TIMOTHY 5:22

There are so many opportunities to be involved in sins of numerous types. They can be sins I commit on my own or sins that others are also participating in. It's a lot harder to find people who truly have a desire to remain pure in every area of life. You don't give us a choice, Father. You've commanded us to keep ourselves pure, and I know that's for our own good. Even though it's not always easy, I want to obey You.

Thank You for putting other godly moms in my life. They face many of the temptations that I face, but they've committed themselves to purity, so together we can encourage one another. What a blessing!

To See God

Blessed are the pure in heart:
for they shall see God.

MATTHEW 5:8

Father, of all the promises in Your Word, this has to be the most amazing. I know that if I am pure in heart I will one day see You. This fills me with awe! But, more precious than this is another truth: You knew that my own heart was anything but pure, so You provided the perfect purification. You sent Your Son to take my wickedness upon Himself and to purify my heart with His blood. It's hard for me to grasp.

I know You loved Your Son far more than I'll ever be able to love mine, yet I can't imagine having my own son take on himself the wickedness of others. What a supreme sacrifice! Oh, how great Your love is for me!

WHATSOEVER THINGS ARE PURE

Finally, brethren, whatsoever things are true,
whatsoever things are honest,
whatsoever things are just,
whatsoever things are pure,
whatsoever things are lovely,
whatsoever things are of good report;
if there be any virtue, and if there be any praise,
think on these things.

PHILIPPIANS 4:8

There's an image of motherhood that is idealistic but not very realistic, Lord. That image shows a perfect lady—always cheerful and helpful, one who never speaks harshly, and one full of wisdom. This all sounds wonderful and too good to be true. The thing is, You do want moms to have these character traits, and we'd be a lot more likely to have them if we were concentrating on pure thoughts.

I know that I tend to get focused on the negatives, and sometimes my thoughts are crowded with impatience, envy, anger, or resentment. I know this is wrong. Please help me focus on You. Fill me with pure thoughts.

TIME OF REFRESHING

*Repent ye therefore, and be converted,
that your sins may be blotted out,
when the times of refreshing shall come from
the presence of the Lord.*

ACTS 3:19

Forgive me, Father. I don't want to do anything wrong; yet sometimes I sin. I'm so sorry, Lord. I feel like the apostle Paul, who said he did the things he didn't want to do. So often my sins are unintentional.

I think of those times when I bathe my children. I don't just wash off the dirt that is visible. I teach them to wash all over for the bits of unseen dirt so that they will be totally clean and refreshed.

At the same time, I teach them that when we pray for forgiveness it isn't just for the wrongs we know we've done. When we repent and You blot out our sins, our burdens are lifted, we are truly refreshed, and our spirits are renewed. Thank You for the opportunity to repent.

TURNING TO GOD

Therefore also now, saith the LORD,
turn ye even to me with all your heart,
and with fasting, and with weeping,
and with mourning.

JOEL 2:12

I have a sin I want to hang on to even though Your Word says it is wrong. I've tried to give it up before, but I ended up snatching it back. What kind of lesson is this for my children if I make excuses for the things I do wrong? What will they learn? They'll believe it's okay to compromise or to dismiss the idea that they are guilty of wrongdoing.

For their sakes and for mine, Lord, I want to turn to You. Just as the prophet Joel did, I want to weep and mourn over my sin—to give it fully to You. Lord, give me the desire to rid myself of the wrong that I'm doing and remind me of Philippians 4:13—that with Your help I can do anything.

LONGSUFFERING LOVE

The Lord is not slack concerning his promise,
as some men count slackness;
but is longsuffering to us-ward,
not willing that any should perish,
but that all should come to repentance.

2 PETER 3:9

Thank You, Lord. You have given me a wonderful example of patient endurance. When I am losing patience with my children, I recall how long You waited for me to repent and turn to You. I was so slow to do that.

Despite my willfulness, You waited for me. You loved me even when I wouldn't acknowledge Your presence, Father. My heart breaks with the weight of my sin against You. I praise You and thank You for being so longsuffering.

Likewise, I want to learn to endure for my children's sake. When they do wrong, I want them to admit it immediately and ask for forgiveness. From Your example with me, I know there are times I need to wait for their repentance. Help me wait, Lord.

HUMBLING AND HEALING

If my people, which are called by my name,
shall humble themselves, and pray,
and seek my face,
and turn from their wicked ways;
then will I hear from heaven,
and will forgive their sin,
and will heal their land.

2 CHRONICLES 7:14

Humble, Lord? Me? Every time I think I'm learning to be humble, my pride gets in my way. I begin to think more highly of myself than I should.

It's even harder to be humble about my children. I love them so much that I want to brag on them all the time. Instead, I need to encourage them but not be boastful, so I won't lead them to be prideful. Finding the middle ground is hard, Lord, but I know You will be faithful to remind me when I get off course.

Thank You for the times I am humbled. You are always here—to listen, to forgive, and to heal. Lord, help me to be repentant, to be willing to be brought low. Heal me, Lord.

FOR THE AGED

*Thou shalt rise up before the hoary head,
and honour the face of the old man,
and fear thy God: I am the LORD.*

LEVITICUS 19:32

There are times when I'm impatient with elderly people. They drive slower. They walk slower. Often they're cranky, and I don't stop to wonder why. I forget how much You understand and love them.

It's not that I don't care; I just don't like to be inconvenienced by them in my life of busyness. Help me determine to put myself in their shoes, to feel the loneliness and the aches and pains that come from aging as their bodies wear out. Give me compassion, so I can show them the respect they need, because I will be there someday.

When I am old, I want my children to respect and love me. By my actions toward others, I am always teaching—either respect or disrespect. I want to set the right example for my children as I honor older people.

FOR MY PARENTS

*Hearken unto thy father that begat thee,
and despise not thy mother when she is old.*

PROVERBS 23:22

Lord, when is it okay to ignore my parents? From Your Word, I see that the answer is *never*. I am to treat them with respect—not because they deserve it, but because You have asked me to. I want to do Your will.

I haven't always wanted to listen to them or obey them, Father—just as I don't always want to listen to You. However, walking my own way isn't showing respect—to You or to them.

Humble me, Lord. Fill me with the desire to hearken to my parents. I can learn so much from them and benefit from their life experiences. I believe this is Your will. Thank You for Your patience and guidance.

OTHER CHRISTIANS

We beseech you, brethren,
to know them which labour among you,
and are over you in the Lord, and admonish you;
and to esteem them very highly
in love for their work's sake.
And be at peace among yourselves.

1 THESSALONIANS 5:12–13

I find myself balking at the thought of anyone, other than You, having rule over me. I want to submit to You alone and not have to listen to other people.

I read about the Israelites in the wilderness. They chafed at Moses' leadership, but, in truth, they were complaining about You, Father. When we complain about those in authority over us, it's the same as murmuring against You. I want to respect You, Lord.

My children must learn to respect authority. In 1 Timothy 2:1–2, Your Word says to lift in prayer our leaders and those in authority and to respect them, because they are Yours. Their rule is not as hard to take when I'm praying for them— for You to guide them. Show me how to encourage peace in my family.

RETAINING HONOR

A gracious woman retaineth honour:
and strong men retain riches.

PROVERBS 11:16

I am such a nag, Lord. I'm sorry for that. I don't want to be that way, but I forget and begin to harp at the children to get the things done that I've told them to do.

I remember hearing a Bible teacher say that after you've told someone to do something three times it's no longer telling—it's nagging. What about after the twentieth time? I'm afraid I might be guilty of this, and I know it isn't teaching my children respect for me, Lord.

If I respect their ability to do what I've asked them, I can quit repeating myself. Then if they don't do as I've asked, they should face the consequences. That way I will retain honor and they will learn to respect themselves and me. Would You be my helper in achieving this?

EACH MOMENT COUNTS

*See then that ye walk circumspectly,
not as fools, but as wise, redeeming the time,
because the days are evil.*

EPHESIANS 5:15–16

Dear Father, it's so easy to put off doing important things—like spending quality time with my children. Sometimes I have the attitude that they're so young it won't matter much if I don't take the time to instill good manners or teach important principles—at least not right now. But they are growing so quickly, and I know that if I don't take the time now to teach them, someone else will, and it probably won't be in the way I'd like or be what I'd want them to learn.

Time is short, so remind me daily to make each moment count. There are so many opportunities to teach them throughout each day. It's my responsibility to use those moments, and I want to take that responsibility seriously. Thank You for being by my side.

THE RESPONSIBILITIES
GOD GIVES

*Having then gifts differing according to the grace
that is given to us, whether prophecy, let us
prophesy according to the proportion of faith; or
ministry, let us wait on our ministering: or he that
teacheth, on teaching; or he that exhorteth, on ex-
hortation: he that giveth, let him do it with simplicity; he that ruleth, with diligence; he that
sheweth mercy, with cheerfulness.*

ROMANS 12:6–8

It's easy, Father, to look at the talents and abilities other moms have and to be jealous because
I'm not as "perfect" as they are. I start dwelling on
how I could have a more immaculate house and
neatly manicured yard. I become bothered that
I'm embarrassing my children because I'm not up
on the latest fashions and their clothes and mine
are out of style.

I fail to remember that You gave me other talents and abilities and You expect me to use them for
Your glory. Those are my responsibilities. I know it's
not wrong for me to try to improve, but it is wrong
for me to let my envy of other moms cloud my
vision. Help me fulfill *my* responsibilities.

SHARING THE GIFT

As every man hath received the gift,
even so minister the same one to another,
as good stewards of the manifold grace of God.

1 PETER 4:10

Heavenly Father, my greatest responsibility as Your child is to share the gift of salvation with others. Your Word makes it clear that this is not an option. You loved me so much that You saved me by Your grace and through faith. Someone who was willing to be a good steward of this gift shared Your gospel with me, so how is it that I sometimes fail to minister this gift to others? Lord, I don't want to be guilty of such neglect!

My family, my neighbors, my children—so many people need to hear Your Word. They all need to have the opportunity to accept You as their personal Savior. Make me attentive to each opportunity You have for me to share Your precious Word with the lost.

GREAT EXPECTATIONS

Unto whomsoever much is given,
of him shall be much required:
and to whom men have committed much,
of him they will ask the more.

LUKE 12:48

Dear Lord, You've given me a life that abounds with rich blessings, and You've guaranteed that because of this You also have great expectations of me. I know that more blessings are in store if I am faithful in the tasks that You've given me. On the other hand, chastisement awaits if I am disobedient to Your call for my life.

I know from experience and from watching my own children that discipline isn't fun; but we all like rewards. I also know I'd rather dole out pleasant things, and I believe that You are like that too.

Help me be faithful to these expectations. Instead of making excuses for why I've failed in my responsibilities, I want to carry them out with joy.

BROKENNESS

The sacrifices of God are a broken spirit:
a broken and a contrite heart,
O God, thou wilt not despise.

PSALM 51:17

I am such a prideful person, Lord. I get caught up in my work, my children, my home, and I forget that without You I am nothing.

Thank You for not forgetting me, Father. You use my trials to show me how much I need You. My heart is breaking. I do want to be broken before You and not the prideful person that is part of my human nature. Lord, I don't want to be someone You would despise. Use my brokenness to help my children learn better how to serve You.

We live in a world that lifts up proud people. Make us all aware of how much You value sacrifice. Help us to have the humble spirit we need when we come before You.

SHOWING MERCY

Go ye and learn what that meaneth,
I will have mercy, and not sacrifice:
for I am not come to call the righteous,
but sinners to repentance.

MATTHEW 9:13

Thank You, Jesus, for calling sinners to repentance. If You had come only for the righteous, I would not have been called, for I am a sinner.

As You have shown mercy to me, help me show mercy to others. There are so many whom I would say don't deserve any consideration. But, I am not the one to make that judgment. Your Word says that we are not to judge. We are to emulate You.

Lord, I have to show compassion for my children and also for strangers. It's easy to show mercy to those who are my own, but sometimes it's hard to have the right feelings toward those who are difficult. You were the best example to follow. You loved everyone, Lord. Help me do the same, and in doing so to set an example for my children.

SACRIFICE FOR ALL

*He is the propitiation for our sins:
and not for ours only,
but also for the sins of the whole world.*

1 JOHN 2:2

I bow before You, Jesus. You, who knew no sin, took on the sins of the whole world. I can't begin to think of the words that are adequate to thank You for Your sacrifice.

Today the children and I talked about heaven and the type of place it is: the purity, the beauty, the perfection. We discussed how You were willing to leave heaven, come to earth, and suffer unimaginable agonies—all so that we would have a way to spend eternity with You.

For myself, Lord, I don't know if I'll ever understand why You made that sacrifice. I feel so unworthy. But, from the depths of my being, I want to shout praise to You and also tell the whole world what You did for all of us.

WITH ALL MY HEART

I will freely sacrifice unto thee:
I will praise thy name, O LORD;
for it is good.

PSALM 54:6

Lord, I can barely talk for the lump in my throat. Tears burn my eyes—not tears of grief but tears of joy and humility. I have been given such a gift today.

You know the trial I've faced. Today I heard my children pray for me. The words were so simple and heartfelt I was overcome, Father. The sacrifice You have allowed me to make in teaching them to talk to You, and follow You, has given them an understanding of who You are. They know You listen to and answer their prayers.

I want my life to be a sacrifice for You, Lord. Help me live a life of praise for You before my children. Guide me in showing them how to make the sacrifice of praise to You.

NONE OTHER NEEDED

*Neither is there salvation in any other:
for there is none other name
under heaven given among men,
whereby we must be saved.*

ACTS 4:12

Jesus. What a wonderful name! It is the only name we need to call upon for salvation. The name given to all people. The only praiseworthy name.

Help me show my children the way to You while they are so eager to learn. They love to hear the Bible stories. They love to pray with me. They love to go to church, but I don't want that to be just to please me, Lord. I want them to have a good foundation in Your Word.

For them to accept salvation, You will need to become real in their lives, though, Lord. I want to teach them about Your grace and mercy—the wonderful gifts You've made available to everyone. I praise You for being the Way, the Truth, and the Life, Lord.

GOD'S JOY

The LORD thy God in the midst of thee is mighty;
he will save, he will rejoice over thee with joy;
he will rest in his love,
he will joy over thee with singing.

ZEPHANIAH 3:17

It's hard for me to apply this verse to myself, Lord. I know that You are mighty and that You save. However, the idea of You being joyful and rejoicing over me is more than I can comprehend.

When I put this in the perspective of my children, though, I get a glimmer of understanding. I look at them and am filled with joy. I love to watch their discoveries and their growth. They are a delight to me, even when they make mistakes.

This is what You want me to see. I am Your child, and You delight in me even when I fall. You pick me up, give me a hug, and encourage me to try again. Thank You for rejoicing over me.

GRAFTING THE TRUTH

*Wherefore lay apart all filthiness
and superfluity of naughtiness,
and receive with meekness the engrafted word,
which is able to save your souls.*

JAMES 1:21

Did You see the mud hole my children made to-day, Lord? They were covered with wet mud from the tops of their heads to their feet. Their clothes were so coated that I threw them aside before washing their bodies.

I thought of this verse as I cleaned my muddy children. I am to cast aside sin as I cast aside their mud-covered clothing. Then You ask me to receive Your Word with meekness. My children don't always face a bath with meekness, yet they always feel, look, and smell so much better afterward.

I want to kick away those filthy habits and embrace the words You have implanted in me, Lord. Please fill me with the words of truth that can save my soul.

A SONG OF SALVATION

Behold, God is my salvation;
I will trust, and not be afraid:
for the LORD JEHOVAH
is my strength and my song;
he also is become my salvation.

ISAIAH 12:2

When my daughter left for her trip today, Lord, I could see the trepidation in her eyes. I knew that she was afraid, so I reminded her of my favorite song from the Scriptures. I sang that song when I was in an uncertain circumstance. The words reminded me of You and Your saving grace, and the melody comforted me. I was reminded to trust in You, Lord.

Because You are my salvation, You truly are my strength and my song. I can sing all day long, Lord. I can teach my children to sing, no matter what is going on around us. I want us to make a joyful noise to You, Jesus, the author and finisher of our faith. We will praise You with every note we sing.

CHRISTLIKE ACTIONS

Put ye on the Lord Jesus Christ,
and make not provision for the flesh,
to fulfil the lusts thereof.

ROMANS 13:14

Dear heavenly Father, so many times when I hear the word "self-control," I automatically think of it as being the opposite of having a temper. Even though that might be true, there is so much more involved.

For instance, in hopes of having a few minutes to accomplish something, it's easy to give in to my kids' pleas for treats, although they've refused to finish their dinner. I know it's a bad idea; it teaches them too many negative lessons (including the lesson that Mommy has no self-control, and if we pester her long enough, we'll get our way).

I know You won't give in and let me have something harmful just because I've asked for it. Help me have enough self-control to use good judgment and make the right choices.

TOO MUCH OF A GOOD THING

Hast thou found honey?
Eat so much as is sufficient for thee,
lest thou be filled therewith, and vomit it.

PROVERBS 25:16

I like to clean and cook and read and cuddle my kids. There's nothing wrong with any of these things. The problem is that I have a one-track mind. I get so involved in one thing that I don't have the self-control to stop and move on to something else when it's time.

I spend time trying to fix a nice meal, even though I should take time to read to my children. Then I become annoyed when they get fussy. I spend hours cleaning, even though my body tells me it's time to take a break with a good book; then I wonder why I'm so fatigued.

Please give me discernment, Lord, to know when I've had enough of one good thing and it's time to move on to the next.

PART OF CHRISTIAN MATURITY

Beside this, giving all diligence,
add to your faith virtue;
and to virtue knowledge;
and to knowledge temperance;
and to temperance patience;
and to patience godliness.

2 PETER 1:5–6

Lord, I really want to grow spiritually. I need to—for my own daily walk with You and for my children and, most importantly, because You've commanded me to. I must be more like You! You've given me a list of characteristics that need to be present in my life for this maturity to take place.

Part of that list is temperance—or self-control. That's really a tough one, Father. There are so many areas in life that require self-control. Sometimes it's hard to keep all of those areas straight, let alone to put this command into practice. I know that You wouldn't have included self-control in the list if it weren't important.

You've promised to give me the strength to fulfill your commands. Thank You for giving me the strength I need to grow spiritually.

A FRUITFUL LIFE

The fruit of the Spirit is
love, joy, peace, longsuffering,
gentleness, goodness, faith,
meekness, temperance:
against such there is no law.

GALATIANS 5:22–23

I've been familiar with the fruits of the Spirit for most of my life, Father. I've introduced my children to them. I've enjoyed many sermons on the subject, as long as the speaker mainly talked about love, joy, and peace. After all, those traits are easy to apply in life—or at least it's easier to pretend they are present.

Temperance? Well, that's a personal matter. It's none of any preacher's business. Right? Okay, Lord, I know that it's conviction I feel when the preacher talks about it. Your Holy Spirit is telling me that self-control is not one of my strengths and I need to work on it. Rather than being offended, help me turn the matter over to You and allow You to develop self-control in my life.

THE SOURCE
OF STRENGTH

*It is God that girdeth me with strength,
and maketh my way perfect.*

PSALM 18:32

O Lord, today is a hard one. I feel like the weight of the world is pressing on me, and I'm not handling it well at all. The kids are fighting. The neighbor wants to talk. I didn't have a chance to have much of a quiet time with You. I feel so weak and helpless.

Quiet my spirit, Lord. Let me close my eyes for a moment and experience Your touch. My strength comes from You, not from any other source. Calm me. Keep me anchored in You and Your Spirit so I will not be dismayed by all that's happening.

Thank You, Lord. When I am resting in You, my family's attitude is different. What a blessing You are to us.

INNER STRENGTH

*That he would grant you,
according to the riches of his glory,
to be strengthened with might
by his Spirit in the inner man.*

EPHESIANS 3:16

I can't believe it, Lord. The trial I am going through should have reduced me to a quivering mess. In my head I know I shouldn't feel so calm. In my heart I only feel peace.

Because of Your strength, Lord, I can smile. I can take my children's hands and stand strong for them. The fear and trepidation can leave their eyes, as they also experience the peace that passes all understanding. I see them begin to relax and trust.

Lord, You don't just shore me up on the outside; You do a complete strengthening of the inside. This is where I need You the most. Let me reflect Your strength so that my children will be drawn to You also. I praise You, Father.

THE PERFECT WAY

*God is my strength and power:
and he maketh my way perfect.*

2 SAMUEL 22:33

You are like an army, Lord, surrounding me with Your strength and power—an army that cannot be defeated. I don't have to depend on my limited might or abilities. You will watch over me.

In these days of wars and fighting, even my children notice the uncertainty around us. When they become fearful, I can tell them how You are mightier than any army. You care for us and will be there when we need You.

In the times when I doubt, Lord, remind me of this verse. Bring it to my memory when I am afraid. Teach me to draw on Your strength and fly above the storm so I can teach the same to my children. Thank You, Jesus.

Lasting Forever

My flesh and my heart faileth:
but God is the strength of my heart,
and my portion for ever.

Psalm 73:26

Time is rushing past me, Father. Some days I feel so old. I don't have the energy I used to have when the children were young. I love my grandchildren, but sometimes I get so worn out when they're here. Physically, I'm wearing out, and it doesn't feel very good.

In the core of my being, in my heart, Lord, I still feel strengthened by You. No matter how slow I've become or how it hurts to get up in the morning, I still want to serve You in any way I can. I can pray for my children and grandchildren during those rest periods I seem to need. I'm grateful for that time. What a blessed promise that this inner strength will be my portion forever.

SHARING AS COHEIRS

If children, then heirs; heirs of God,
and joint-heirs with Christ;
if so be that we suffer with him,
that we may be also glorified together.

ROMANS 8:17

What blessing! What joy! To be an heir of the living God, the Maker of the universe. I stand amazed to be called a joint heir with Jesus—the Savior and Messiah for all who believe. This is a glorious promise that is almost too much to grasp.

In the midst of suffering, I sometimes forget the gift You've given me. I focus on myself. I overlook who You are and what You are doing for me. It's even harder when someone in my family is suffering. Then my discomfort is increased.

I want to keep my eyes on You, Jesus. The suffering You endured for my sake makes my trials look like nothing. Help me look forward to the promise, to forget the temporary troubles I have now.

THE EXAMPLE OF CHRIST

What glory is it, if,
when ye be buffeted for your faults,
ye shall take it patiently?
But if, when ye do well,
and suffer for it,
ye take it patiently,
this is acceptable with God.

1 PETER 2:20

I didn't do anything wrong, Lord. You know that, but it seems as if everyone else is against me. This isn't fair. I want to make them understand what they have done to me.

Why should I accept the suffering for something when I did nothing wrong? Yet, You tell me to take it patiently—that this is acceptable to You. Why, Lord? Verse 21 says it's because of Your suffering and the example You set for us.

Perhaps my children will be accused of wrongdoing when they are innocent. Help me to encourage them by showing them this truth in Your Word, Lord—that we will also suffer. Thank You, Jesus, for giving us this truth.

BEING BLESSED

Blessed are ye, when men shall revile you,
and persecute you,
and shall say all manner of evil
against you falsely,
for my sake.

MATTHEW 5:11

How can I do this, Lord? How can I be blessed when people are upset with me because I believe in You? I keep thinking of the way this is affecting my children. I want them to see their mother as a godly woman, but if they begin to doubt, then what? Help my children understand the need to suffer persecution for Your sake.

When I put this into perspective, Lord, I know You suffered much more persecution than I am now. Although tempted, You made the right choices. You didn't deserve what was done to You.

Keep me strong in my faith, no matter what. When I am following You, I can be blessed, no matter what others say about me. Thank You, Jesus, for mapping the way for me and for my children.

EXCEEDING JOY

Rejoice, inasmuch as ye are
partakers of Christ's sufferings;
that, when his glory shall be revealed,
ye may be glad also with exceeding joy.

1 PETER 4:13

There will come a day, Lord, when Your glory will be revealed. This earthly life will come to an end. I will be in heaven with You.

What a joyous time that will be! Scripture promises there will be no more pain, no more tears, no more suffering. I can't begin to imagine what that will be like, but I look forward to that time with intense longing. The greatest joy will be sharing that time and place with You, Lord.

I must remember that my children's suffering is every bit as real to them as mine is to me. I need to be compassionate, to show them that they are facing exceeding joy because of these trials. Thank You, Jesus, for allowing us to partake of Your sufferings.

WITH DILIGENCE

*Thou shalt teach them diligently
unto thy children,
and shalt talk of them when
thou sittest in thine house,
and when thou walkest by the way,
and when thou liest down,
and when thou risest up.*

DEUTERONOMY 6:7

O Lord, this is wonderful! You don't want me to lecture my children constantly on Your ways, but I can fit in tidbits of truth, no matter what we're doing.

There are so many comparisons to Your statutes in everyday life. Help me see those and convey them in a real way. At times my children are so eager to learn; other days they would rather not listen. I want to make You exciting and interesting to them. Give me creative ideas as we take walks, clean the house, do schoolwork, or engage in other routine duties.

Your ways are awesome, Lord. Teaching my children can be a burden or a delight. The choice is up to me. I pray it will be a delight for all of us.

GRACE AND JOY

Let the word of Christ
dwell in you richly in all wisdom;
teaching and admonishing one another
in psalms and hymns and spiritual songs,
singing with grace in your hearts to the Lord.

COLOSSIANS 3:16

What is in my heart? Your Word says that out of the heart can come evil if we're not careful. Fill my heart with Your love, so that my teaching will reflect You, Lord.

I don't want my children to be subjected to worldly teachings when they are at home; they get enough of those when they are away from me. Give me wisdom, Lord. I want to teach them Your Word so that we can teach and admonish one another with Scripture.

When our hearts are full of You and Your Word, then we can sing with grace and joy. My children and I can proclaim Your goodness to all those we meet. That way the teaching will continue on to others around us. What a blessing!

PARENTAL INSTRUCTION

My son, hear the instruction of thy father,
and forsake not the law of thy mother.

PROVERBS 1:8

They don't listen to me, Lord. I get so angry. I know I should be firmer with my children and make them mind me. The problem is that when they look at me with those soulful eyes my desire to discipline melts away.

What am I teaching them by doing this? That's the problem. By allowing such leniency, I am giving them the idea that they don't have to abide by the rules. When they are grown, they might believe that You don't require them to follow Your absolutes.

Give me wisdom and strength in my instruction to my children. Help me to be firm when I need to be, yet tender and giving as the teaching allows. Guide me in how to show love for You and Your laws, Lord.

SOUND DOCTRINE

*Speak thou the things which
become sound doctrine.*

TITUS 2:1

Thank You, Father, for giving us sound doctrine.
I have boundaries set by You that I can follow and
teach to my children. We don't have to wonder
what's right and what's wrong. All we have to do
is look to You and Your Word for guidance.

Guard my tongue as I teach them, Lord. Don't
let me say foolish things that will confuse or lead
them astray. Instead, let my words be a constant
reminder of the way You want us to walk. Season
my speech with grace—to encourage my children
and remind them to walk in Your path.

I praise You, Lord, that Your Word is a light for
us to follow, a lamp in the darkness of this world.

PROTECTION
FROM CORRUPTION

*But I fear, lest by any means,
as the serpent beguiled Eve through his subtilty,
so your minds should be corrupted
from the simplicity that is in Christ.*

2 CORINTHIANS 11:3

Drugs. Smoking. Violence. Foul language. Illicit sex. Lord, these are only a few of the temptations facing my children in today's world. Peer pressure is so strong and difficult to resist. Satan is seductive as he tries to lead Your children away from You.

Please protect them, Father. I can't be with them all the time. I've tried to instill godly values, to arm them with the spiritual armor they need, but the enemy is a deceiver. Send Your Spirit with them. Bring to their minds the Scriptures they've memorized. Keep them from being corrupted and led away from Your truth.

Lord, as Abraham placed Isaac on the altar of sacrifice, I place my children before You. Protect them, Father. Thank You for keeping them in Your care.

Jesus Understands

*In that he himself hath suffered being tempted,
he is able to succour them that are tempted.*

Hebrews 2:18

Lord, sometimes I feel like no one knows or cares
what I'm going through or the temptations I'm facing. But then I read Your Word and feel ashamed
of how wrong I am. You chose to come to earth
and live as a man so that You could understand
the trials we face and be able to help us make the
right choices.

Help me remember the temptations I faced as
I was growing up. I want to understand my children the way You understand me. I don't want to
be judgmental or give them the idea that I am
better than they are. I see so many parents who
don't try to see things through their children's
eyes, and who are not sympathetic with the trials
they face. I don't want to be like that. Help me be
like You, Lord.

BEARING THE BURDEN

There hath no temptation taken you
but such as is common to man:
but God is faithful, who will not suffer
you to be tempted above that ye are able;
but will with the temptation also make a way
to escape, that ye may be able to bear it.

1 CORINTHIANS 10:13

In the garden, Lord, You prayed to have the cup of suffering taken from You. You understood sorrow, temptation, and all that we suffer here on earth. Yet, You also said, "Not my will, but thine, be done" (Luke 22:42).

This burden is heavy, Lord. There are days when I don't know how much longer I can go on. I try to hide this from my children so they won't hurt too, but sometimes I can't. The choices they make in their own lives may depend on the way I handle this trial.

Your Word says that You will provide a way of escape. You help us carry our burdens. There are others who have carried this same weight before me. I want to lean on You, Father. Then I can teach my young ones the joy of being able to trust in You.

Being Able to Stand

Wherefore take unto you
the whole armour of God,
that ye may be able to withstand in the evil day,
and having done all, to stand.

Ephesians 6:13

Many temptations come from evil forces that are so deceptive they are hard to see. The devil fights against us. I see his subtlety in the ways my children are tempted by their peers and the influences of society to do wrong. I'm not immune to it either, Lord.

Thank You for providing a way that we can be protected from the full assault of Satan's deceitful lies. I have told the children how You've covered us with protection from the top of our heads to the soles of our feet. All we have to do is make the decision to put on the armor You've given. When we are properly dressed in Your protective covering, we can stand against any temptation, no matter how deceptive.

LET MY CHILDREN
SEE MY THANKS

We thy people and sheep of thy pasture
will give thee thanks for ever:
we will shew forth thy praise to all generations.

PSALM 79:13

I have so much to be thankful for: my family, a home, the salvation of God. My list of blessings is never ending.

Lord, may I never fail to praise You and to thank You for the many blessings You have given to me. I pray that my children and their children and each successive generation will understand that all the glory belongs to You. Without You we would be nothing and would have nothing.

Thank You for Your love and faithfulness to us. Thank You for making us Your people and for allowing us to be the sheep of Your pasture. Thank You for allowing us to serve such a great God!

SO MUCH
TO BE THANKFUL FOR

*In every thing give thanks:
for this is the will of God in Christ Jesus
concerning you.*

1 THESSALONIANS 5:18

Father, Your will is for me to be thankful, no matter what. It's easy when days are bright and spring is in the air. I feel so alive on those days. It's harder when the days are dreary. I feel more sluggish and grumpy, and apparently my children do too. They whine and fight and drag out every toy in the house, looking for something to do.

It's not as easy to be thankful on those days, Lord, but You said it's Your will. If I think about it, I do have much to be thankful for on those days. For one thing, I have my children. I also have You strengthening and teaching me. On those dreary days I want to learn to rely on You more. Thank You, Lord.

THANK THE FATHER

*Giving thanks unto the Father,
which hath made us meet to be
partakers of the inheritance
of the saints in light.*

COLOSSIANS 1:12

Thank You, God, for cleansing me of my wickedness and allowing me to come out of the darkness of sin and into the light of Your salvation. If I had nothing else for which to be thankful, that would be enough. I'm so blessed to be one of Your saints. Thank You, Lord, that so many of my friends and family members have also found this new life in You.

I'm grateful that I have the opportunity to teach my children the truths that are found in Your Word. I'm trusting that You will open their spiritual understanding. I am looking forward to the day that they will accept You as Savior and be "partakers of the inheritance of the saints in light." From that day forward I will have something else for which to thank You.

MORE REASONS TO BE THANKFUL

I thank thee, and praise thee,
O thou God of my fathers,
who hast given me wisdom and might,
and hast made known unto me
now what we desired of thee.

DANIEL 2:23

Father, like Daniel, I thank You for answers to prayers. In my life, these answers are many. You've said "yes" to my request for a husband and children. You've given me wisdom as You promised. You've provided financially and physically, even when the situations seemed impossible. It is wonderful to know I have a God who delights in hearing and answering my prayers. I am glad to be able to give thanks.

I want my heart to continually be filled with praise and thanksgiving to You. Keep me anchored in the thought that all You do is for my good and for Your glory. Only You are deserving of my praise and adoration. Accept my heart—a heart that is full of thanksgiving!

WITH THE WHOLE HEART

*Trust in the LORD with all thine heart;
and lean not unto thine own understanding.*

PROVERBS 3:5

Lord, I want to trust You. I give all my cares to You and try to walk away, but so often I fail. I begin to reason with myself. Then I begin to fear and doubt. I snatch back all my cares, as if I am more trustworthy than You.

Forgive me, Lord. I don't want to do this anymore. I want to trust You completely—with my children, with my life. Letting You have total control is easy to say and so hard to do. I feel like I'm walking in the dark, not knowing which way You're leading us.

That doesn't matter, though. I know I can trust You with my whole heart. You alone are worthy. I give it all to You, Lord.

BLESSING AND HOPE

Blessed is the man that trusteth in the LORD,
and whose hope the LORD is.

JEREMIAH 17:7

Blessed. Trusteth. Hope. What wonderful words those are, Lord. Through study, I know that blessed means a refuge. You bless me by being my shelter, my protector, and my hope when all seems hopeless.

Verse 8 tells about this person who trusts You being like a tree planted by a river. Those trees receive the sustenance they need, even in the dry times. You are a source of nourishment for me, Lord. I want my roots to go deep and to be well watered by You.

As my children grow, I need to treat them like young trees, planting them firmly in Your Word. Then, as I see them getting stronger every day, Father, I pray that they will trust You, experience that hope, and be blessed.

EVERLASTING STRENGTH

Trust ye in the LORD for ever:
for in the LORD JEHOVAH is everlasting strength.

ISAIAH 26:4

How long is everlasting? A million years? A billion years? I can't even comprehend that length of time. My time is measured in hours, days, years, and sometimes even in minutes. The thought of everlasting is so vast that I can't understand it. Explaining eternity to my children is almost impossible.

I can trust in You, Lord, because Your strength never fails. It is there for all eternity. You don't weaken like I do. You are omnipotent.

The heroes my children admire today have weaknesses. But not You, Lord; You are perfect. Your strength is everlasting. I want my children to trust You as their only hero—their all-wise, all-powerful, all-sufficient, mighty protector—the One they can trust in forever and ever. I praise You, Lord.

PERFECT PEACE

Thou wilt keep him in perfect peace,
whose mind is stayed on thee:
because he trusteth in thee.

ISAIAH 26:3

Perfect peace. Lord, we live in a world of turmoil. There doesn't seem to be any peace from the small neighborhood to the international level. Fighting. Wars. Bombs. Threats. How can there be any tranquility found anywhere? No earthly army can protect us from harm.

Yet, this verse promises that when we trust in You we will experience peace. The peace that passes all understanding is ours for the asking. Despite wars and rumors of wars, our reliance on You can bring unexplainable contentment.

Lord, I explained peace to my children today as being a core of calm deep inside. No matter what happens to upset us on the surface, You are in our innermost being, bringing peace and comfort. Thank You that we can always trust You.

THROUGH GOD'S WORD

Through thy precepts I get understanding:
therefore I hate every false way.

PSALM 119:104

O Lord, lazy people want everything handed to them. They want life to be easy and to get everything they need. They don't want to work for anything. To my shame, I am that way sometimes. But through Your Word I get understanding. It implies that to have the knowledge I need I must work at learning. Without studying Your Word I won't understand what You want from me, Father.

How can I show my children Your ways unless I teach them from the Bible? They have to learn the basics just as I have: Working is good; being lazy is not acceptable.

Help us to be diligent in understanding You and Your precepts. Please give me a continuous desire to know You better.

BEING PEACEABLE

*He that is void of wisdom
despiseth his neighbour:
but a man of understanding
holdeth his peace.*

PROVERBS 11:12

I don't want to have understanding, Lord. My neighbor deliberately did something to hurt my children. I have every reason to have hard feelings toward this person. I want to take care of this myself. The anger feels good.

I want to rant and rave, to tell my children what a rotten person this neighbor is. But Your Word says we are to return cursing with blessing. Just like You treated those who beat You and put You to death, I am to forgive those who mistreat my children.

This is so hard, Father. I know I have to place them in Your hands, but I don't want to. Give me the strength and ability to hold my peace and show my children the proper behavior. Give me understanding. Help me to see this person through Your eyes.

BROUGHT TOGETHER IN LOVE

That their hearts might be comforted,
being knit together in love,
and unto all riches of the
full assurance of understanding,
to the acknowledgement of the mystery of God,
and of the Father, and of Christ.

COLOSSIANS 2:2

Comfort my heart. Give me full understanding and assurance. In this family of Christ, I should be feeling rich in love and compassion. Instead, some of the people are critical of me or of my children, and that hurts, Lord.

To be honest, there are many times I'm critical too, and I'm reminded that it is my pride that usually causes me to criticize others. These people are my family, Lord. By finding fault in them, I'm setting a poor example of how to belong.

True love is kind, not prideful or self-seeking. Fill me with compassion for my fellow Christians so I might be a godly example of love and understanding. I want to emulate You, Jesus.

WITH EVERYTHING IN ME

*Wisdom is the principal thing;
therefore get wisdom:
and with all thy getting get understanding.*

PROVERBS 4:7

In this verse You say to get something, either wisdom or understanding. You mention wisdom as being principal—of utmost importance, Father.

I told my children that getting wisdom means to be obedient to the rules and statutes You give us, Lord. Only when we are obedient can we truly get an understanding of who You are. With everything in us, we should strive to be wise and to know You in all Your glory and power.

Help me show my children the need to be self-controlled, to not give in to the temptation of sin. Only when we turn from sin can we truly get an understanding in all wisdom. We need an infusion of Your strength to help us reach for this goal.

OVERCOMING THE WORLD

*For whatsoever is born of God
overcometh the world:
and this is the victory that
overcometh the world,
even our faith.*

1 JOHN 5:4

I don't feel victorious. I don't feel as if I've overcome the world. Instead, the world presses close; temptations and troubles abound. My faith seems so weak—not the type of faith that might bring victory.

You don't say our faith will overcome *if* we feel up to it. You say everyone who is born of You will overcome. I can teach my children this principle: Our victory doesn't depend on how we feel; it comes from knowing You and depending on Your power and might.

I want to stand up and shout. V-I-C-T-O-R-Y. In You I have the assurance of victory. The world doesn't stand a chance. I've read the story, and in the end all evil will be thrown down. You will reign victorious. I praise You, Lord.

MORE THAN CONQUERORS

*In all these things we are more than
conquerors through him that loved us.*

ROMANS 8:37

What utter joy, Lord! Through You I have no reason to fear. Through You I have complete victory, even in the times when I don't feel victorious. I can ignore those feelings of defeat.

Today there are so many forces in the world that are coming against my children and me. Romans 8:38–39 goes on to say that there is nothing in heaven or on earth that can separate us from Your love; nothing that has happened before or that is yet to come can separate us. What wonderful reassurance!

I can remind my children of this every day in our devotion time. There is nothing ahead that they need to fear. Because of You and Your sacrifice, we have victory. We are more than conquerors through You, Lord.

THANKS TO GOD

Thanks be to God,
which giveth us the victory
through our Lord Jesus Christ.

1 CORINTHIANS 15:57

This language I speak is so inadequate to tell You what I want to say, Lord. I can't begin to find the words to thank You for the many successes I have in my life. You are awesome, Lord.

The victory this verse speaks about is so amazing. I pointed out to my children that we don't have to rely on our own abilities or the abilities of others; we only have to wait on You, Lord. You are the mighty One—the One who helps us triumph over the world.

There is no condemnation for us when we believe in You, Jesus. The covering of Your blood helps us to prevail over anything. We never need to fear anymore. Thank You for giving us this victory.

A HEAVENLY VICTORY

*To him that overcometh will I grant
to sit with me in my throne,
even as I also overcame,
and am set down with my Father in his throne.*

REVELATION 3:21

Lord, Your Word promises me a place in heaven with You. Not only that, but I will be seated with You in Your throne. I don't understand how that can happen, but I'm humbled and awed by the promise.

Overcoming isn't something I can do on my own, Lord. Without my encouragement and example, my children won't be able to avoid doing wrong things and stick to the right. When I show them and tell them about Your ways, then they will become victorious as they learn more about You.

There may be certain times when I need You and Your Word to guide me. Lead me, Lord. Help me become an overcomer. I look forward to sitting with You in heaven.

ABUNDANT WISDOM

If any of you lack wisdom,
let him ask of God, that giveth to all men liberally,
and upbraideth not; and it shall be given him.

JAMES 1:5

God, without question, I lack wisdom. Each day I am faced with numerous decisions, and there are questions for which I have no solid answers. I have to make discipline choices. I have to decide if my children need to see a doctor. I wonder how warmly I should dress my children. Is the latest toy or game safe for them?

Then there are long-term questions, such as what method of education is best for our family. And these are questions mainly about my kids. They don't even touch on other important decisions. We also have family decisions, such as what method of transportation is best? How can we have quality time together, despite our busy schedules? How much money can we save?

Lord, it all seems overwhelming to me. Please give me the abundant wisdom You've promised, and help me to relax in the knowledge that You will guide me.

SPEAKING WITH WISDOM

The words of a wise man's mouth are gracious;
but the lips of a fool will swallow up himself.

ECCLESIASTES 10:12

Time and time again I've heard the saying, "It is better to remain silent and let people think you a fool than to open your mouth and prove it." There's a lot of truth in this quote, Father. You said something similar in Your Word.

I'm ashamed to admit that I often forget these truths. I speak before I think, and the words that come out of my mouth are anything but wise. My children must think it strange when I'm so preoccupied with something that my responses to them make no sense. That's only one example of speaking before thinking. Sometimes what I say to others is hurtful. Your Word says to be gracious.

I want my children to be wise enough to think first, then speak. Please help me be their example.

SPIRITUAL WISDOM

For this cause we also,
since the day we heard it,
do not cease to pray for you,
and to desire that ye might be filled with
the knowledge of his will in
all wisdom and spiritual understanding.

COLOSSIANS 1:9

Dear God, as much as I need Your wisdom in the daily decisions I must make concerning my family, I need it even more for spiritual matters. Although I've been around the truths of Your Word most of my life, I still have questions and much to learn. As I read and study Your Word and hear sermons preached about it, give me a clear understanding of what You are saying to me through it.

I want the wisdom and ability to apply Your Word in my life, and I want to use it to teach my children. I know it is Your will for me to understand Your Word, and You've given me the Holy Spirit to guide me. I pray I will take advantage of this great blessing.

WORDS OF WISDOM

She openeth her mouth with wisdom;
and in her tongue is the law of kindness.

You've made it plain that one requirement for being a virtuous woman is that the words I speak be graced with wisdom and kindness. I know this means that I must be careful how I speak, not only to my children but also to my husband and to others.

It's not always easy. In fact, many times my human response is to react with quick and foolish words that I will eventually regret. Only when it's too late do I stop to consider the effect my words have had.

O God, help me think before I speak. Put words of kindness in my mouth that will build up others instead of destroying them. My desire is to be a virtuous mother.

No Need to Worry

The LORD is my light and my salvation;
whom shall I fear?
The LORD is the strength of my life;
of whom shall I be afraid?

PSALM 27:1

Dear God, what tremendous faith the psalmist had! It's hard to imagine not being afraid when a person has enemies like the wicked and powerful ones that David had. But David remembered his strength and salvation were in You.

Lord, as a mother, I've often found myself afraid. I worry about the things my children will face in this world. I get concerned that I really don't know how to be a good mother. There are so many things that tempt me to fear.

Please forgive my weakness, Lord Jesus. Help me remember where my strength and salvation come from and to say with David, "Whom shall I fear. . . . Of whom shall I be afraid?"

TRUST IN GOD

*What time I am afraid,
I will trust in thee.*

PSALM 56:3

What familiar words these are, Father. I memorized these words when I was a child in Sunday school. My teachers taught me to apply them to childhood fears I might face: thunderstorms, darkness, dentists. I guess many people look at this as a Scripture just for children.

I do want my little ones to begin applying this principle at a young age, but I want them to understand that they can carry it with them into adulthood. It helped me when I went from a small high school to a big college. It gave me strength as I entered the career world. It encouraged me when I embarked on the marriage journey. And it gave me boldness to enter a life of motherhood.

These words are very power filled. I commit myself to applying them daily.

GIVE IT ALL TO GOD

*Casting all your care upon him;
for he careth for you.*

1 PETER 5:7

Lord, if I trust You for my eternal salvation, why don't I trust You for my daily needs? If I were honest, I'd have to say that I know I can do nothing about my salvation other than accept You. However, when it comes to my daily concerns, I often feel there's something I can and should be doing.

A lot of it has to do with my children. I feel that if I don't worry about them and do something about it, they won't turn out right. I know that in reality my job is to pray daily for them and bring them up according to Your Word. Then I must totally give them to You and trust You to work in their lives.

Instill in me the peace that comes from casting all my cares on You.

One Day at a Time

*Take therefore no thought for the morrow:
for the morrow shall take thought
for the things of itself.
Sufficient unto the day is the evil thereof.*

Matthew 6:34

Often I think I'm going to drive myself crazy as I allow worry after worry to pile up. Father, I try to convince myself that it's just healthy concern for my family, but in my heart I know better. I know it's nothing short of worry, and Your Word tells me it shouldn't be part of my life.

I should "take. . .no thought" about anything. There are enough constructive things for me to do each day, and worrying consumes so much energy. It seems to affect every area of my life, and it deflates my joy. It harms my relationship with my husband, my children, and others.

Lord, I don't want worry to overtake my life. Help me to give my concerns to You and to concentrate on the work You have for me.

Prayers & Promises